World of WINDOWS

World of WINDOWS

Any remodeling project starts with inspiration and imagination. Here's a visual portfolio of great ideas that will delight your eyes and tickle your fancy.

THE COVER

An elegant arrangement of Pella® windows and doors creates a stunning, light-filled room.

What architectural style will your new home be? Colonial? Modern? New Victorian? This section will show you the many possibilities and great diversity of styles being built on the American landscape.

Here are ways to organize your creative thoughts and ideas to make sure your building or remodeling project fulfills your needs.

Windows and doors will be some of the most important elements in your project designs. Here's what you'll need to know to create beautiful, well-proportioned exteriors and interiors.

Express your ideas effectively to architects and other experts.

Page 8

Clear communication between a Midwest couple and their architect made a dream house come true.

Page 53

Page 50

Page 30

Page 61

Page 118

*T*hink about a beautiful sunrise, about how the sun lifts over the horizon and fills the world around us with light and hope. Planning a remodeling or building project is like the beginning of a new day. It is the start of exciting and challenging opportunities. It is a chance to express your most creative ideas, and a time to build a better and brighter way of living for you and your family.

At the Pella/Rolscreen Company, we understand how important your home's future is to you. That's why we created this exceptional book. It contains a wealth of practical information to help you achieve your goals, and inspiring photography to spark your imagination. Use this book to plan for the wonderful changes ahead, and to discover the many ways that fine Pella® products can give your dreams lasting quality.

FRAMING
YOUR VISION

Windows and doors are extraordinary architectural elements. They blur the distinction between indoors and outdoors, and permit your home's interiors to merge with the world around you. Windows and doors extend your vision and expand your home.

The placement of windows and doors should be a primary consideration of any building or remodeling project. Look to frame views that are especially pleasing: A moss-covered oak; city lights sparkling in the distance; a clear view of your children at play in the backyard. This concept is so important that we've given it a name. We call it Windowscaping® design. You'll call it beautiful.

AN INSPIRING VIEW OF WASHINGTON, D.C., IS POETICALLY FRAMED IN A PELLA® FULL-CIRCLE WINDOW WITH CUSTOM WINDOWPANE DIVIDERS.

PRECIOUS LIGHT

The many kinds of light that enter your home create moods, warmth, and a wonderful sense of livability. With careful planning, you can take advantage of light's many personalities.

Eastern light is the morning's gift. It is soft and cheerful, perfect for breakfast nooks, kitchens, or the bedrooms of early risers. Southern light can be strong. In winter, when the sun sits low on the horizon, southern light becomes the essence of solar-home design.

Western sunsets are spectacular, but summer sun from the west can be hot. Plan shades or awnings for west-facing windows. Northern light is diffuse and even—the artist's light. Take advantage of it with skylights.

FALL SUNLIGHT STREAMS THROUGH SOUTH-FACING PELLA® CASEMENT AND CIRCLEHEAD WINDOWS IN THIS SOUTHWESTERN ADOBE HOME. A WELL-PLACED OVERSTUFFED CHAIR CREATES A COZY RETREAT FOR READING OR DAYDREAMING.

8

BEAUTY BY DESIGN

indows and doors should be beautiful. They should harmonize with the design of your home, architectural details, and the placement of your furnishings. They should be an expression of your finest creative ideas.

Our products not only look great, they perform beautifully as well. Each Pella® window and door exceeds the industry standards of quality. Every Pella product is designed for easy maintenance and superior endurance, and offers the most advanced energy-saving technology.

A commitment to excellence means the best value for you and your home. That's why our windows and doors are Built to Impossibly High Standards. Our Own®.

PELLA® CASEMENT AND QUARTER-CIRCLE WINDOWS FLANK A TRADITIONAL FIREPLACE AND MANTEL IN A BEAUTIFUL DISPLAY OF ARCHITECTURAL HARMONY.

10

WORLD OF IDEAS

REMODELING AND BUILDING PROJECTS ARE AS VARIED AS the people who design and build them. Each one differs in size and complexity, and each is designed to fulfill certain dreams and hopes. To help you imagine the possibilities, we've prepared a photographic portfolio of many fine remodelings and newly constructed homes. It's a world of ideas at your fingertips, and one of the ideas may be just right for you.

BRILLIANT REMODELINGS

THE OWNERS OF THIS STONE HOME *ABOVE, RIGHT,* AND *LEFT,* TRANSFORMED A SCREENED-IN PORCH INTO A SUN-FILLED FAMILY ROOM. THEY ENCLOSED THE PORCH BY FITTING PELLA® CUSTOM ARCH-HEAD CASEMENT WINDOWS INTO EXISTING OPENINGS.

Remodeling has become an American way of life. We delight in exploring ways to increase the livability of our homes, and good old Yankee ingenuity abounds in the way we alter, expand, and open up our personal environments.

Our remodeling instincts give us many reasons for change. We may reconfigure walls or modify floor plans so that areas of our homes become more comfortable or functional. Often, we look for ingenious ways to create additional living space to accommodate our growing family. Perhaps we simply want to refresh our older, outdated rooms with newer materials, colors, and sources of light.

More American families than ever are deciding to remodel their homes instead of moving away from familiar, established neighborhoods and schools. As a result, spending on home improvements has more than doubled since the early 1980s. Americans spend more than $100 billion every year on remodeling projects that include everything from repainting bedrooms to building multiroom additions. Remodeling has become an established industry that features state-of-the-art products and techniques. Families either do the work themselves or hire expert professionals who specialize in remodelings.

Most important, today's homeowners enjoy significant roles in their home's future as decisionmakers, designers, and even part-time builders. This increased involvement strengthens our emotional ties to our homes and creates the opportunity to specify finely crafted, quality components like Pella® windows and doors to add lasting value for years to come.

ADDING A LIGHT TOUCH

Adding windows to a home is one of the most popular of all remodeling projects. It is a simple, low-cost way to open up your home to light, views, and ventilation without major changes to structural members.

ENLARGING
WINDOW SIZES
BRINGS THIS
SITTING AREA TO
LIGHT, *OPPOSITE.*

REDESIGN YOUR
LIVING ROOM
WALL WITH
CUSTOM ARCH-
HEAD WINDOWS AT
RIGHT.

A BRIGHT SPOT
WAS CREATED
WITH CUSTOM
WINDOWS AND
LEADED GLASS
OVER AN ENTRY
DOOR *BELOW.*

Adding a box-bay window above a kitchen sink, installing a casement window in a dark stairway, or placing a circlehead window over an entry door are examples of how window remodelings can add design flair and create new horizons for your home. Think about including a skylight if you'd like to open up an attic, kitchen, or family room without disturbing walls or the arrangement of cabinets. A skylight is an excellent way to add light to a bathroom and maintain privacy.

The Pella/Rolscreen Company has a huge selection of windows and doors to match your unique style and vision. If our wide array of standard products isn't enough, we also make custom windows to

BANISH DARKNESS
AND WELCOME
THE LIGHT WITH
AN INVITING
SKYLIGHT, *LEFT*.

OPEN YOUR ATTIC
TO POSSIBILITIES.
PELLA® CUSTOM
WINDOWS,
OPPOSITE, CAN
MATCH THE SLOPE
OF ANY ROOFLINE.

AN ELLIPTICAL
WINDOW LENDS AN
ELEGANT TOUCH
TO A SIMPLE
SECOND-STORY
BATH, *BELOW*.

any specifications. All of which means that there are no limitations upon your imagination. If you can visualize it, there will be a Pella® product to fulfill your dream.

NEW LIFE FOR OLD ROOMS

If you are searching for ways to increase living areas, don't overlook parts of your home that already exist. An underused area such as a basement or attic can be finished with wall, ceiling, and flooring materials to provide an extra family room or bedroom. With a little imagination, a tucked-away nook can become your home office, or an old walk-in storage closet can turn into that much-needed extra bathroom. Because these types of remodelings usually don't involve changes to structural walls and often use heating and cooling systems already in place, they can be a cost-effective way to increase the livable square footage of your home.

Windows and skylights are essential when it comes to reviving underused areas. They add light and vitality to your finished

**QUALITY PELLA®
PRODUCTS MADE
THIS RESTORATION
LEFT ENERGY
EFFICIENT AND
HISTORICALLY
ACCURATE.**

**A REPLACEMENT
BOW GRACES THE
DINING AREA
*ABOVE.***

rooms, and they are important design elements. With the right touch, a window can transform any room into extraordinary space. For example, you may have decided to install a pair of casement windows over the tub in your modest new upstairs bathroom. Go ahead and include an elliptical window over those casements and voilà! Your little bathroom takes on a character and personality all its own. Pella® Circlehead windows are made to match the width of many stock window sizes, and the Pella Custom Plant can manufacture just about any window or door system you can imagine. Don't forget that all Pella windows and doors are designed to meet the highest quality standards.

WORTHY REPLACEMENTS

A remodeling project doesn't have to create extensive changes or add large amounts of space in order to enhance the livability of your home. By replacing old windows and doors, you can beautify

your home and vastly improve its thermal energy performance. You won't have to worry about changing the size of window openings, either. The Pella® Installation System is designed to make any replacement project quick, easy, and economical, so that a new window can be fitted to virtually any opening.

A replacement project can be an expression of your creativity, too. Try removing a bank of older windows and replacing them with a beautiful Pella Bay or Bow. The change will be dramatic, and you'll be amazed how a bow or bay window can magically increase your living area.

The Pella Installation System is especially important for projects of historical significance. It allows you to install maximum quality and energy efficiency without sacrificing character. Across the country, this flexible system has met very demanding local and national guidelines for renovation and restoration. In addition, the Certified Pella Contractor program is available nationwide. CPC members are expert building professionals who have been specially trained in the techniques necessary to install any Pella product.

The Architect Series™ line of Pella products was developed to meet the special challenges of remodeling older homes. These exceptionally beautiful windows and doors are a remarkable blend of advanced technology and old-world craftsmanship. They were created to satisfy

architects, builders, and homeowners who insist on high performance but want to maintain the historical accuracy and integrity of their renovation projects. The Architect Series™ recalls the dignity and beauty of mission, prairie, French colonial, and other timeless architectural styles.

ELOQUENT DOORS

One of the best ways to increase living area is to gain access to the out-of-doors. Today's nature-loving families like to while away warmer days on a deck or patio, and there is no finer place for relaxed entertaining and casual conversation. In fact, decks and patios are some of the most popular of all home improvement projects. By adding either a sliding glass,

EXTEND YOUR LIVING SPACE WITH GLASS DOORS *ABOVE* AND *RIGHT* THAT OPEN TO A DECK. ADDITIONAL FIXED UNITS CREATE WALLS OF LIGHT.

PELLA® LOW-MAINTENANCE EXTERIOR CLADDING, *LEFT*, LOOKS BEAUTIFUL AND LOCKS OUT THE ELEMENTS.

ONLY 3 FEET WAS
NEEDED TO BUMP
OUT THE WALL OF
A LIVING ROOM
AND CREATE THE
STUNNING GLASS
SUN SPACE AT *LEFT*
THAT INVITES THE
OUTDOORS INSIDE.

EXTENDING A
WALL 10 FEET
DOUBLED THE SIZE
OF THIS KITCHEN
RIGHT AND
ALLOWED PLENTY
OF WORK SPACE.
THE 8 × 10-FOOT
OPENING IN THE
CEILING HAS
PELLA® SKYLIGHTS
AND FIXED
WINDOWS TO
BATHE THE ROOM
IN LIGHT FROM
ALL DIRECTIONS.

a French sliding, or a traditional French door, you can make a graceful transition from indoors to your outdoor retreat.

BUMPING OUT, ADDING ON

Bump-outs, the little remodelings that go a long way, can bring big changes to your home's interior for relatively modest cost. Bump-outs push out portions of existing walls no more than 3 or 4 feet, yet they can alter traffic patterns, provide valuable extra seating, and bring enormous amounts of welcome light to the interior.

Full-scale room additions and second-story additions are major projects, and the remodeling process may last for several months. A complete kitchen overhaul can be a complex and expensive endeavor. Regardless of the size or scope of your project, however, remember that good design and careful planning are keys to success.

Explore the next chapters of this book to find great advice and information on designing, planning, and how to make your own project a source of pride and satisfaction for years to come. □

BRIGHT, NEW BEGINNINGS

Building a new home is an American dream. It is one of the most exciting challenges you'll ever have, and the day that you finally move in provides a thrill that lasts a lifetime. A new home can create powerful emotions. It is an expression of yourself, your personality, and the all-important needs of your family. For some, it is a culmination of life's goals.

The new homes of the 1990s are a blend of style and practicality. Contemporary building methods and state-of-the-art materials ensure that today's homes are more beautiful, energy efficient, and maintenance-free than ever before. Thanks to a wealth of consumer information available in books

AT HOME IN MOST REGIONS OF THE COUNTRY, THIS CONTEMPORARY FARMHOUSE *TOP LEFT* FEATURES AN INVITING FRONT PORCH.

LOW ROOFLINES AND TALL WINDOWS, *BOTTOM LEFT,* DISTINGUISH THIS VERSION OF A CLASSIC PRAIRIE-SCHOOL DESIGN.

A JOYOUS PROFUSION OF WINDOW STYLES SHOWS THAT THE OWNERS OF THIS HOME *RIGHT* ARE INDEPENDENT THINKERS WITH A SENSE OF WHIMSY.

PELLA® OCTAGONAL AND CIRCLEHEAD WINDOWS PROVIDE ACCENTS FOR A VICTORIAN-INFLUENCE DESIGN, *OPPOSITE*.

CUSTOM WOOD WINDOWPANE DIVIDERS SET A TRADITIONAL TONE FOR A NEW ENGLAND COLONIAL, *RIGHT*, AND A SPANISH COLONIAL, *BELOW*.

THE INTERNATIONAL STYLE *ABOVE* DEVELOPED IN THE 1920S. THIS MIDWESTERN VERSION HAS ROUNDED CORNERS, WOOD SIDING, AND A DISTINCTIVE ROUND WINDOW.

and magazines, modern buyers are increasingly savvy. They are better informed about the choices ahead, and are more apt to be an integral part of the decisions that will affect their lives for years to come.

SAY IT WITH STYLE

One of the first and most enjoyable choices facing the would-be home builder is the matter of architectural style. The possibilities are limitless. Traditional or contempo-

rary? Prairie-school influenced, classic saltbox, or a house that is just as eclectic as you are? A photographic portfolio, such as the one in this chapter, can give you a visual tour of house styles that is both informative and delightful, permitting you to sample a world of differences.

Often, architectural styles are regionally based. For example, many saltbox homes are found in the Northeast. Prairie-school architecture comes from the Midwest, and adobe still is a common building material in the Southwest. When selecting just the right home, consider investigating the regional architectural styles in your area. Although regional styles often migrate to all parts of the country, you may wish to know if your house will be strikingly different from those around it. Appropriate architectural style can help your home retain its value and appreciate at the same rate as other homes in your neighborhood.

Remember that many new housing developments have restrictions or covenants that require your house to meet certain

RANCH-STYLE HOMES ARE ALWAYS POPULAR. THIS NEW HOUSE IN CONNECTICUT AT *LEFT* HAS A LIGHT-GATHERING CLERESTORY COMPOSED OF PELLA AWNING WINDOWS.

A HOME IN THE PACIFIC NORTHWEST, *LEFT,* PRESENTS A QUINTET OF FRONT-FACING GABLED DORMERS. PELLA® CIRCLEHEADS OVER DOUBLE-HUNG WINDOWS LEND A TRADITIONAL TOUCH.

A MIDWESTERN STONE COTTAGE, *RIGHT TOP,* AND A CALIFORNIA SPANISH COLONIAL, *RIGHT BOTTOM,* EXEMPLIFY THE INFLUENCE OF REGIONAL STYLES.

design criteria. If a distinguished style is your preference, you may find that a private wooded lot or other secluded location allows you some design flexibility. For more information about selecting a location and buying a lot for your new home, see pages 72–75.

Plan books are another great source of home styles. These books are sometimes available on the newsstand or are advertised in home-type magazines. They offer a variety of stock house plans, often grouped according to the size of the house, and the plans can be purchased through the book publisher. Kit or precut houses are also popular, and most manufacturers of kit or precut homes feature a variety of styles from which to choose.

PICTURE THE FUTURE

Today's professional architects and home builders identify a number of trends that will influence new-home construction for the next several years. One such trend is the downsizing of homes near urban centers. In these areas, land available for new home developments is scarce. As a result, lots are increasing in price and shrinking in

TRADITIONAL WINDOWPANE DIVIDERS AND CLAPBOARD SIDING HELP BRING A BIT OF CAPE COD TO THIS MIDWESTERN COTTAGE AT *LEFT.* ADOBE HOMES OF THE SOUTHWEST, *OPPOSITE,* ARE STRONGLY REGIONAL.

STRONG, BOLD LINES OF A CONTEMPORARY HOME, *BELOW,* CONTRAST WITH THE QUIET DIGNITY AND CLASSIC LOOK OF A NEW BRICK COLONIAL, *BOTTOM LEFT.*

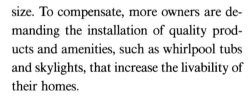

size. To compensate, more owners are demanding the installation of quality products and amenities, such as whirlpool tubs and skylights, that increase the livability of their homes.

New homes will also emphasize architectural detailing, such as dramatic woodwork, built-in bookshelves, and sculpted ceilings. Open floor plans will reflect casual life-styles and enhance the sense of spaciousness for smaller homes. Imaginative use of windows and glass doors will turn homes into light-filled castles.

Pella® windows and doors make ideal components for today's new homes. A huge selection of standard or custom products provides a wealth of architectural character, and their superior construction meets every expectation of quality. If your new home deserves the very best, it deserves Pella products. □

BRING YOUR IDEAS TO LIGHT

THESE ARCH CASEMENT WINDOWS *LEFT* ARE FROM THE PELLA® ARCHITECT SERIES LINE OF PRODUCTS. THE CUSTOM-MADE WOOD WINDOWPANE DIVIDERS ARE STRIKING RE-CREATIONS OF GOTHIC-REVIVAL STYLE.

WHEN VIEWED WITH AN ARCHITECT'S EYE, A SIMPLE STAIRCASE, *RIGHT,* CAN BECOME A FLOWING SYMPHONY OF LIGHT AND LINES.

NOW, GATHER UP YOUR BEST IDEAS AND TURN THEM INTO reality. To help you begin, we offer a fascinating chapter about designing your building or remodeling projects. Explore your creativity, encouraged and inspired by expert advice from professional architects and designers. Learn how the pros think, how they visualize the final results, and what steps they take to ensure success. Then begin designing with windows to create your own masterful project.

I suggest people begin by making a scrapbook of their favorite things, to help communicate the images and ideas that are in the mind's eye. A good design process starts with what you know and understand, then expands it and goes beyond it, so that you end up with something more wonderful than you ever imagined.

—Melanie Taylor
Architect, New Haven, Connecticut

IMAGINE THE POSSIBILITIES

Building or remodeling a house gives you a rare chance to shape your home according to your needs, preferences, and imagination. Even if you are working with an architect or other design professional, you don't have to adapt yourself to someone else's ideas. Instead, you can tailor every aspect of your project to reflect your own style and tastes, to fit the way you live, and to fulfill your definition of comfort.

This chapter will help you make the most of the wonderful opportunities a building or remodeling project can offer. You'll learn to:

■ tap your creative instincts to determine the features and functions you want in your home.

■ imagine the possibilities for using light and views to enhance the beauty of your living spaces.

■ communicate effectively with design professionals—architects, designers, and builders—to translate your ideas and dreams into final plans.

SETTING YOUR GOALS

Planning a home is like working a puzzle. You choose the features and functions you want, then fit them together bit by bit to form a final picture. The process can take time, but careful design planning is always worth the effort.

The first step in planning is to develop a list of what you want from the space

you are building or remodeling. Ask each member of your family to create a wish list, using the questions below to stimulate their thinking. Then, sit down, compare answers, and list your goals in order of priority. The planning process presented in this chapter will help you refine these goals and make them more specific. When you're done, you'll have a solid set of objectives to share with your architect or builder.

Here are questions to consider.

■ **How will I use the space?** Every space should suit the activities that will take place there. Write down how your family will use each room for work, play, and relaxation every day. Also think through how you might use the space for special occasions, such as when you entertain or prepare for holidays. Then, translate those needs into features through the "if, then" process of thinking: *If* the children will play in the family room, *then* I need storage for toys and surfaces that are easy to clean. *If* we want to host formal dinner parties, *then* we'll need room for a table that can seat 12. Also list the furnishings you'll need to make the room work comfortably.

■ **What special features spell "comfort" to me?** If you've always wanted a six-burner commercial gas range, a circlehead window, or a laundry room near the linen closet, add those elements to your wish list. Consider what you like most about your present home; write down those features, too.

■ **How will my needs change over the coming years?** Small children thrive on wide-open family spaces, but they may want more privacy when they're teens. A step-up tub platform could present tricky footing as you age. By thinking about future needs, you can build in flexibility: you could dig a basement and finish it later for the kids, or add a walk-in steam shower next to the tub.

■ **How should the space I'm planning relate to the rest of the house?** Everyone knows that it makes sense to have a dining room near the kitchen. Other decisions are more personal: Do you want the master bedroom near the kids' area? Do you want to see into the kitchen from the family room? Be explicit about how the spaces should interact.

■ **How should the space I'm planning relate to the outdoors?** Plan to make your yard an extension of your home's living area. Think about how a new deck might provide additional space for outdoor family dining or how a patio could give you a quiet spot for sunning. Consider where you'll need French or sliding doors for easy access to the yard.

DEFINING YOUR STYLE

One of the rewards of building a new home is getting a house that reflects your personality. Undoubtedly, you already know what you like: whether your tastes run to the traditional or the contemporary, whether you prefer an eclectic mix or a particular style. The challenge lies in putting together design elements that bring your personal style to life in a pleasing and original way.

To prime your imagination, stock up

KEY CONCEPT:
The Right Connections

With today's fast-paced life-styles, more families are planning homes that foster togetherness and relaxed living. Floor plans put a premium on open spaces designed for a variety of activities. Examples: kitchens that connect to family rooms; family rooms with access to outdoor entertaining centers; master suites with areas for reading and exercising.

More than a bedroom, a master suite is a full-fledged living space. In the suite *below*, the right connections include a fireside sitting area and a luxury bath. *Your* retreat might include a dressing room, an exercise room, or a private patio.

Connect a kitchen breakfast nook to a deck with French doors or sliding glass doors, *right*. You'll enjoy a sunny setting for everyday meals, plus convenient access for dining alfresco.

I *see a trend away from dark interiors to a more light, airy, spacious, informal feeling. I think that, across the country, life-styles are getting more informal. When informality comes, the spaces open up and the relationship between the indoors and outdoors grows in importance.*

—**Mike Kephart**
Architect, Denver

on design magazines and books. Tour model homes and browse through the showrooms of furniture, plumbing, and kitchen suppliers. Visit The Pella Window Store® to see different window and door styles.

Document things you like by saving magazine pages, brochures, and samples. On each photo, jot down what appeals to you. Be specific: "I like the blue marble counter on the vanity" or "Love that elliptical window over the bath!" As your research progresses, you'll find your design goals growing clearer. If you're working with an architect or designer, you can use these pictures to show the look and features you want.

CREATIVE VISUALIZATION

Identifying the basic pieces of your design is one thing. Putting them together so they form a coherent whole is another. That's why hiring a competent design professional makes good sense for major projects. Whether or not you choose professional help, however, your creative urges and personal preferences are important. You'll need to be able to express your ideas so that your finished project works well for you and your family. Use the following techniques to visualize how your ideas can fit into a cohesive plan.

■ **Scheme on paper.** Drawing floor plans helps you test your design ideas on paper. If you are building a new house, your first sketches may simply show the relationship between rooms and the rough proportions of each. If you're remodeling, however, it's worth the time to develop a scale drawing of your home. Then, you can put tracing paper over the

plan and try out possible changes.

To make scale drawings, you'll first need to measure the rooms you are remodeling. Use a 25-foot tape measure to measure length and width. Also measure the size and location of doors, windows, fireplaces, and other fixed architectural elements. Using these data, draw your plan to scale on ¼-inch graph paper; use one square to represent a foot. Also show the location of important outdoor elements, such as the big oak tree you want to save or the swing set you want to see from the kitchen window. Check your local building codes to determine how far additions must be set back from the street or neighboring properties; note these restrictions on your plan.

Once your drawing is complete, consider the options for reworking the layout: mentally move walls, relocate doorways, and redefine the function of rooms. Imagine adding new elements such as bump-outs, room additions, windows, doors, and built-ins. Sketch potential changes on your tracing-paper overlay. Add scale drawings of your furniture. Then, pencil in arrows to show how traffic will flow through the space.

Now, critique your plan. Is there enough room for all the furniture you need? Is there at least a 2-foot traffic lane around furniture? Will traffic avoid work or conversation areas? Is there room for doors to swing and chairs to pull out from tables? Does the plan fulfill your goals?

■ **Give ideas dimension.** Floor plans can clarify a layout, but they don't answer the question, "What will it look like?" For that, you need to draw wall elevations—a view of each wall straight on. In addition to the measurements from the floor plan, you'll need the floor-to-ceiling measurement (if the ceiling slopes, measure at several places to establish the slope). Draw to scale the size and position of windows, doors, and fixed elements, such as fireplaces.

Planning on paper doesn't cost a thing, so experiment with your boldest ideas, from big window groupings, to fanciful fireplace surrounds, to specialized built-ins. When you've completed your sketches, imagine how the room will look. What will you see as you stand in the doorway? What will you see through the windows? How will the room look from each corner?

To see how changes will look from the outside, you can draw exterior elevations. Or, have a photo of your home's exterior enlarged to 8 × 10 inches. Then, use tracing paper and sketch changes over the top. Ask yourself if the new facade is balanced and well proportioned and if the new elements work well with the old.

■ **Build a model.** To see a room in three dimensions, transfer the floor plan and elevations for all four walls to cardboard. Tape the pieces together to form a model. Some home-center stores carry kits for making multiroom models.

■ **Try it life-size.** If you're adding on to a house, you can get a sense of the space by laying out its boundaries in your yard. Use clothesline or string and stakes to show where the room will go. You can "furnish" the space with lawn furniture or cardboard boxes. If you're remodeling a room, use peel-away masking tape (available at paint stores) to mark doors, windows, and built-ins on the wall where they might go. □

KEY CONCEPTS:
Attention to Detail

People today want big, airy rooms, but with the little details that say home: wood moldings, beautiful built-ins, elegant windows, and well-planned views from room to room. Consider using special ceiling treatments, such as a tray or coffered ceiling, to make tall rooms feel more intimate. Or, try small touches of marble or other rich materials to dress up a space.

The art of architecture: Ascending floor levels and carefully aligned openings set up a pleasing rhythm, *below*, while the repetition of white and wood helps tie the levels together. Vignettes like this are the reward of meticulous planning.

A homey hearth, wide wood moldings, and glass-door cabinetry add to the comforts of a big, daylighted family room, *right*. Even though the space is large, the seating area is intimate and the mood is inviting.

People today don't want dull,
ordinary, look-alike homes.
They're putting more emphasis on
combining windows in dramatic
groups or placing them in a very
balanced, formal arrangement to
help create the character
of a room.

—Jack Bloodgood
Architect, Des Moines

DESIGNING WITH WINDOWS

As you dream the possibilities for your home, you'll probably find your imaginings filled with windows. That's natural, because windows make a powerful design element: They can literally shape a room's character out of light, line, and thin air. The styles and shapes of your windows, their sizes, where you place them, even how you dress them—all these factors help weave the ambience of your home.

Whatever your mind imagines, you can achieve with Pella® windows and doors. You can choose from literally hundreds of standard sizes and shapes to bring out the special qualities of your home. You can also combine standard windows and doors or have units custom-made to achieve designs that are uniquely your own.

SETTING YOUR STYLE

Inside your home and out, windows are a fundamental element of style. From the exterior, windows work with other architectural building blocks—the shape of the house, roofline, and materials—to establish your home's architectural style. Just as important, windows dictate character on the inside. Along with interior detailing and finishes, windows set the stage for furnishings, art, and accessories.

Because windows are part of the permanent architecture of your home, it's important to choose window styles that will create exactly the character you're after. Every window style—double hung, casement, or custom—projects a different personality.

Double-hung windows with wood windowpane dividers, for example, convey a traditional feeling, whether you march them across the front of a formal Georgian home or set them in pairs for a country cabin. Clear expanses of glass—casements or fixed-pane windows—express a clean, unbroken line that's usually associated with contemporary architecture. Diamond windowpane dividers are the stuff of storybook styles, such as Tudor, French eclectic, and Cotswold cottage. You can finesse the mood of a window by where you place it or how you treat it, but its underlying personality will still come through.

If you are building a new house, your architect and builder—and the experts at The Pella Window Store®—can help you make window choices that enhance the overall architecture of the house. If you are remodeling a home or replacing windows, you'll probably take cues on window style from your existing home. The innovation comes in how you combine and place the windows.

Once you've selected your basic style, let your imagination soar. Make windows bigger, line them up in threes and fours, pop them into unexpected places, or stack them to two-story heights. The simple goal is to use windows—and the light they bring—as a

memorable design element within your home. As you dream the possibilities, consider all the roles windows can play.

LETTING IN LIGHT

Regardless of your home's style, light will bring out the best in your interiors. You don't have to create clean white rooms to enjoy sunny living. Sunlight will polish the natural tones of woodwork or play up the rich hues of dark colors. If you're remodeling,

nothing will rejuvenate your home more than bright new sources of light and air.

Plan your window design to bring in generous amounts of light. Keep in mind that the more directions from which you draw light, the more complex and beautiful your light will be throughout the day. For rooms you live in day in and day out, it's nice to draw light from three or more sides. Think, for example, about the friendly feeling of a family room wing that has south, east, and west walls, with windows on each. Or,

TRIPLE GABLES, EACH PIERCED BY A WINDOW, LIFT THE FARMHOUSE *ABOVE* TO NEW HEIGHTS. AT NIGHT, THE GLOW MAKES A WARM BEACON TO HOME.

consider setting a breakfast room into a sunny five-sided bow. Although not every room can be surrounded by light, keep in mind that skylights, bays and bump-outs, jogs, and other design tricks can help you vary the source of daylight entering a room.

Light that comes predominantly from one side will have a more distinctive character. Southern and eastern windows, for example, will let in a buttery, warm sunlight. Indirect light from the north tends to be cooler, and western light is harsher. You'll want to take these qualities into account as you decorate your room. For example, warm colors—colors with red and yellow undertones—can make north-facing rooms feel cozier, while icy pastels, cool blues, and gray-greens will tone down overly strong sun from the west.

In some cases, you may want to let light into a room without admitting a view. The scenery outside may be unsightly—a detached garage or a house that's close by. Or, you may just need privacy. Skylights are a classic choice for such situations, but you can also get creative: Place windows high on the wall, or cluster small windows in an attractive design.

As you plan windows, look for ways to funnel light into the interior of your home, so the whole house is bright. Here are some ways to share the wealth.
■ Use glass, rather than solid walls, to partition space. Install French doors between rooms, or use dividers of glass block or etched glass.

A WALL OF PRAIRIE-STYLE WINDOWS FROM THE ARCHITECT SERIES™ SETS THE CHARACTER OF THIS HOME. EVEN SPARSELY FURNISHED, THE ROOMS HAVE THE BEAUTY OF SURE PROPORTION AND ABUNDANT LIGHT.

Windows generally need to be bigger than people expect. With today's energy-efficient windows, you can get tremendous delight from selecting window sizes that provide expansive views and good amounts of light. There's something about having that friendly sunshine as part of your inside life—it gives you a good payback over the years.

—Steven B. Haines, Jr.
Architect, San Francisco

■ Cut away a portion of solid wall to form partial walls, pass-throughs, interior windows, or transomlike openings.

■ Install a second-story skylight over the stairway to brighten a first-floor hall.

BRINGING THE OUTDOORS IN

A gracious home doesn't dead-end at the exterior walls. Instead, it uses windows and doors to make a gentle transition to the outdoors. Often, it connects physically to the outdoors as well, with glass doors that step out to patios and decks, to landscaped courtyards or tranquil lily ponds.

To make the most of outdoor assets, place your windows where they will command the most desirable views. If you have a lovely backyard, for example, choose large windows that let you savor its beauty. Or, compose a whole wall of windows and doors. A wall of windows gives a room a special quality: It blurs the distinction between inside and outdoor space, so you feel as if you are literally living in the outdoors.

You can use outdoor features to enhance your Windowscaping® design. You might create a landscape focal point, such as a grove of small trees or small fountain, to draw the eye outside. Also consider repeating interior design elements in your outdoor plan. For example, add an arched trellis that mimics the shape of your circlehead window, or paint the deck railing in a color you pick up from inside. These small touches knit together the indoor and outdoor space.

Indoor/outdoor connections are equally important at the front of the house, especially around your entry. Transoms and sidelights at the front door will fill your foyer with light and give you pretty glimpses of the outside. At night, the transparent space gives off a welcoming glow that makes a wonderful introduction to your home.

OPENING UP SMALL SPACES

Windows make space look bigger simply because they don't stop your eye—they let your view extend to the outside. You can manipulate a home's interior views to take advantage of that fact. For example, you might position French doors in your family room so they line up with the doorway to the foyer. That way, when guests enter your home, they'll be treated to a space-stretching view through the family room and out the French doors.

If your space is small, be especially conscious of planning landscape features outside important windows. These exterior focal points trick the eye into seeing past the boundaries of the house, so the space looks larger. You can also expand rooms with windows that add depth—such as a Pella® Bow or Bay Window. Just replacing a small window with a larger window or glass doors will make a room feel more open.

ENHANCING YOUR INTERIOR DESIGN

Windows play an integral part in the interior design of your home. A shapely window or window grouping has the visual clout to serve as a room's decorative focal point. When you trim a window with lovely woodwork and frame a pretty view, you've essentially created a permanent and living piece of artwork on your wall. Focal-point windows make special sense in small spaces; they make for beautiful viewing without dominating the room or eating up valuable floor space.

Not every window has to be a focal point, of course. You can also use windows as small architectural gems—the round window you place in a dormer, for example, or a circlehead set about a tub. Just the way you trim and treat a window can make it a memorable complement to accent your decor.

In addition to their visual impact, windows influence the way you arrange a room and how you use it. As you plan your interiors, think carefully about how your windows and furniture will work together. Here are some factors to consider.

■ Plan windows to leave adequate wall space for major furniture pieces. For example, you may want to leave an uninterrupted section of wall for a media center in your family room, or plan a "bed wall" in your bedroom.

■ Position windows so sill heights work with your furniture. Sills should be high enough to accommodate any chests or bureaus that must go beneath them.

■ Take into account future window treatments. If you love ruffled country curtains for the bedroom, you might be happy with single or paired windows instead of larger groupings. If you want elaborate cornices, leave enough space above the window to accommodate them.

■ Make sure furniture arrangement and window placement work together to let you enjoy good views. When you plan a

KEY CONCEPT:
The Important Window

Windows today are more than background players. They often are the decorative focus of a room, with designs that emphasize shape and form as much as light and view. Important windows can also be delightfully deceptive, by making small spaces feel more open. Make one beautiful window the centerpiece of a room, or combine several in a Windowscaping® design.

Windows make welcoming entries, such as the one *below*. Inside, they deliver light and design interest. Outside, they offer inviting glimpses of what waits within. In the evening, your whole home will seem to glow from the lights inside.

The new hearth: Mix the solid comforts of the fireplace *right* with the sheer drama of glass. Today's prebuilt fireboxes, with their compact flues, invite you to dabble in geometry. You could even surround a fireplace with glass.

spectacular window wall, for example, allow room for a sofa where you can sit and appreciate the scene outside. If you put a bank of windows in the dining room, extend them low enough so you can see out when you're sitting down.

When you plan furnishings and windows together, you open up all kinds of intriguing design opportunities. Use windows as natural spotlights for your treasured objects: "Cap" a four-poster bed with a shapely transom window, or flank an heirloom breakfront with window sidelights. If there's a special piece you'd like highlighted, factor that into your planning from the outset.

DRESSING YOUR WINDOWS

As design tastes have moved to bigger, more decorative windows, window dressings have put more emphasis on the windows themselves. Many windows are lovely enough that they require no dressing at all. If you prefer a softer look, however, graceful treatments such as balloon shades, swags, and lace panels can put color and pattern at the window without hiding the architecture. Even with elaborately dressed windows—such as traditional drapes with cornices—you can still let light and window show through. For example, you can mount your cornice mostly above the window so that it doesn't block light. Make drapes wide enough that, when they're opened, they won't obscure the windows.

With many Pella® windows and doors, you can choose shading options

A COMBINATION OF PELLA® DOORS AND WINDOWS STRETCH THREE STORIES TO CREATE THE FEELING OF A ROOM IN THE WOODS. WINDOWPANE DIVIDERS AND WOOD MOLDINGS GIVE THE BIG ROOM ELEGANT DETAIL.

People today are looking for the joyousness of light, bright rooms. In many cases, we're decorating with minimal window coverings to maximize the light coming into the room. Or, I'm using no window treatment at all, just good-looking trim around the window. That's why it's important that the window be beautiful.

—**Beverly Ellsley**
Interior Designer, Westport, Connecticut

that are right for today's light look: Pella® Slimshade® blinds or Pleated Shades. Slimshades are slatted blinds that fit between the inner and outer panes of the window's double-pane glazing system; Pleated Shades use accordion-pleated fabric between the panes. The shades or blinds can be closed to control light or privacy. Opened, they almost disappear. You can combine Slimshades or Pleated Shades with other window treatments, or leave your windows untreated for a clean, architectural look.

Here are some tips for treating different types of windows.

■ **Single windows.** Well-proportioned Pella windows look lovely with any simple treatment. For a fuller look, use curtains in a classic style—tiebacks, colonial tabs, café curtains, or panels hung from rings. For a more vertical line, use floor-length curtains.

■ **Matching groups.** With three or more windows in a group, you can dress each window individually or treat the group as a single design element. If you are using individual treatments, keep them simple.

■ **Bays and bows.** These shapely windows look pretty with top treatments that follow the window frames. Or, treat them as one element by mounting your treatment on the window alcove.

■ **Circlehead windows.** Minimal is the word. Consider soft, flowing treatments that emphasize the window shape.

■ **French doors.** Shirred panels mounted on each door are a classic privacy treatment. If you simply want softness, try a swag mounted above the door frame, where it won't interfere with the door's operation. □

A SUNNY SWAG, *OPPOSITE,* LETS LIGHT, VIEW, AND THE BEAUTY OF THE WINDOW SHOW THROUGH. FOR A SOFT TOUCH, THE FABRIC PUDDLES ONTO THE FLOOR.

SLIMSHADE® BLINDS, *BELOW,* CONTROL LIGHT AND PRIVACY.

*E*ven if a homeowner has clear
ideas about what each room
should look like, it's not an easy
process to make those spaces fit
together in an attractive package.
It takes someone like an architect
to sift through the needs and
ideas expressed by the owner and
develop a cohesive design.

—Tom Baldwin
Architect, Des Moines

WORKING WITH THE PROS

No matter what the size of your project or your budget, you can find competent design help to fit your needs. There are many types of design professionals, and most offer many different levels of services.

ARCHITECTS: RESPECTED DESIGN PROS

Architects are highly respected members of the design community. They are well educated in all aspects of creative planning, and their expertise includes site planning, structural engineering, and problem solving. In addition, architects must pass rigorous tests to become registered by the state. This extensive educational and testing program helps ensure that the consumer obtains a quality design.

An architect offers comprehensive design capabilities. A full-service package includes planning your project, preparing the working drawings for construction, specifying all materials to be used, and supervising construction. However, you have the option of requesting a more limited design package—omitting construction supervision, for example. You can also hire an architect for spot assignments, such as consulting with you on an hourly basis about your project.

For full services, an architect may charge a flat fee, or an hourly rate with a guaranteed maximum. Either way, the architect's involvement will add about 10–15 percent to the cost of your project. For smaller projects, expect to pay on an hourly basis.

DESIGNERS AND PLANNERS

There are a variety of design professionals that can deliver high-quality work. In some instances, they are able to take on small projects where an architect's fee might be prohibitive.

■ **Design/build firms** offer services similar to those provided by architects. They are popular because they build the projects they design. As a result, their fees are usually reasonable.

■ **Space planners** are also called building designers, architectural designers, or remodeling planners. These pros will develop a design concept for your project and, if you wish, draw working plans. Fees are often based on an hourly rate, generally less than that of an architect.

■ **Interior designers** take on the complex job of dressing your space: developing color schemes and selecting furnishings. If involved early in the process, some interior designers can help plan your entire project. They charge by the hour, by fixed fee, or by marking up the wholesale prices of furnishings.

■ **Certified Kitchen Designers** have passed tests given by the National Kitchen and Bath Association. They often work for cabinetry showrooms, which offer their services for free or at a low cost.

■ **The Pella Window Store**® offers trained specialists who can help you plan Windowscaping® designs at no charge. See page 71 for more information about The Pella Window Store.

PICKING THE RIGHT PRO

To identify good candidates to design your project, get recommendations from friends or from professional societies, such as the American Institute of Architects or the American Society of Interior Designers. Interview three or four candidates. Discuss the individual's education and experience, your needs and budget, and fees. After the interview, call client references and visit several examples of the person's work. Check candidates' records with the Better Business Bureau.

Be sure you are comfortable communicating with the individual you choose. If you feel that your ideas are not being appreciated, keep looking.

SPEAKING FREELY

At the first meeting with your design partner, share the planning tools you've developed: your goals, the photos you've clipped, and your sketches. Keep in mind that this material only represents the first step of the planning process. A good architect or designer will want to understand your ideas and goals, then take a fresh look at how to fulfill them. For instance, there may be structural limitations that make your plans very expensive. Your design pro may suggest a less costly alternative. A good architect will be especially adept at dealing with potential problems and developing alternatives that fulfill your goals.

PLANNING YOUR DREAM HOME

As the design of your home or remodeling evolves, you'll have ample opportunity to share your ideas, respond to sketches from your architect, and participate in choosing materials for your home. Most architects, and some building designers, use the step-by-step design process outlined below.

DEVELOPING THE PROGRAM
Your architect will meet with you and your family to become thoroughly familiar with your goals, your life-style, and your building budget. He or she will also evaluate your building site or, for remodelings, your home and yard. From these steps, the architect develops an understanding of all the factors that need to be addressed by the design. This is called the "program" for your project.

REVIEWING SCHEMATICS
Your architect will develop schematics, or simple drawings, of one or more designs that fulfill the program. At a review meeting, you'll see basic floor plans and get an idea of the proportion of the rooms. At this stage, your options are wide open, so comment honestly on any aspect of the plan. If you are uneasy with the design of certain rooms or the project as a whole, say so. Also, if you have

your heart set on specific kinds of materials or products, such as quality Pella® Windows and Doors, this is the time to convey your wishes.

DESIGN DEVELOPMENT
When you are satisfied with a general approach, your architect will start developing the details. This process can take weeks or months, depending on the scope of the project. Along the way, you'll see more specific floor plans and perspective drawings of important spaces. You'll also review increasingly refined sketches of the exterior, such as the one *above*. (Turn the page to see how the house looked as built.) For big projects, you may see a cardboard model. As you sign off on the basics, such as the form of the room and the placement of windows, the process shifts to the details such as cabinetry layout and design of built-ins.

PREPARATION OF WORKING DRAWINGS
Your architect will prepare working drawings that show the contractor exactly how to construct the design. These plans include specifications for all materials, from structural lumber to mechanical systems to the finishes. Look these specifications over carefully to ensure that all the materials and products you have requested are part of the plan.

Working with an architect rewards you with a home that's tailored for you. Bill and Sue Conyers (shown **above** with daughter Chris) went to the drawing board with architect Tom Baldwin (seated) and got just the house they wanted—a shingled charmer cozy enough for two, but big enough to welcome a family.

A CASE STUDY

Some people might label the shingle-and-stone home *right* traditional. Some might look at its wide wood trim, circlehead windows, and entry columns and call it postmodern. Ask owners Bill and Sue Conyers about their home, though, and they don't talk architectural style: They talk life-style.

"This is the first house we have ever built for how we live every day instead of how we *think* we might live," says Bill. Drawing upon their prior experience with building and remodeling, Bill and Sue knew exactly what they wanted to achieve, and they shared every idea with architect Tom Baldwin. "The house reflects our lifestyle," says Bill. "Tom made something aesthetically pleasing and satisfying out of it."

Although Baldwin had previously designed the couple's vacation home, Bill and Sue took nothing for granted in expressing their needs. Sue came to the first planning meeting with a scrapbook of magazine photos she had clipped. Bill brought a checklist of special systems he wanted included, from a gas-condensing furnace to a dumbwaiter. They both brought firm ideas about the type and style of space they needed.

Baldwin's design reflects the couple's ideas inside and out. On the exterior, Bill and Sue wanted the house to look like the shingled summer houses they had admired along the New England coast. Although the Conyerses live in Des Moines, far from the ocean, Baldwin agreed that the rustic style would work well on the couple's wooded, sloping lot. His design incorporates classic elements of the shingle style: irregular, sculpted shapes, columns and arches, intersecting cross gables, a

THE CONYERSES' HOME COMBINES SHINGLES, STONE, AND BEAUTIFUL WINDOWS IN AN EXTERIOR THAT'S TRADITIONAL YET RELAXED—MUCH LIKE THE COUPLE THEMSELVES.

contrasting trim band, and, most notably, a rusticated stone base below wood shingle siding. A Pella® Circlehead window serves as the visual focal point for the front facade.

Inside, the Conyerses requested a house that could lead a double life. Their five children are grown, so Bill and Sue wanted everyday living spaces that are suited to a newly quiet life-style. At Christmastime,

however, the house swells with children and grandchildren. Those occasions call for a place that can handle a crowd.

Through a series of meetings, Baldwin and the Conyerses hammered out a floor plan that responded to both sets of needs. The plan creates two types of living areas on the main level: To one side of the central entry, a formal living room runs the full depth of the house, providing a

spacious area for family gatherings and parties. To the other side lies a casual living zone, with a kitchen, den, breakfast nook, and sun porch. A dining room links the formal and informal zones at the back of the house.

Bill and Sue wanted open and airy interiors. Baldwin responded with tall ceilings (10 feet in the living room), and floor-to-ceiling Pella windows. An unobstructed

FORMAL BUT GRACIOUS, THE LIVING ROOM *LEFT* TAKES WARMTH FROM TALL WINDOWS, A CROSS-BEAM CEILING, AND AN INTIMATE SEATING AREA.

THE DINING ROOM *OPPOSITE* OVERLOOKS A WOODED BACKYARD. THE ROOM'S WHITE, BLACK, AND WOOD DESIGN THEME CONTINUES IN A MORE CASUAL MODE IN THE KITCHEN *BELOW*.

floor plan allows sight lines and conversation to flow easily.

The casual side of the house has the smaller, more intimate spaces Bill and Sue live in every day. Says Sue: "On winter evenings, we like to curl up with a book in front of a fire in the den. In our old house, we had a huge family room, but it was too big, especially as our family got smaller." For this house, Baldwin designed a small den with a corner fireplace and a pass-through to the kitchen. "I'm crazy about this little corner we have as our family room now," says Sue. "With the kitchen right here, this has become the hub of the home for family and friends alike."

Finishes and furnishings help distinguish the home's formal and informal spaces. The living room represents the home's formal side. Painted woodwork, a beamed ceiling, subtle color, and traditional sofas and chairs set the tone. Bill and Sue planned a place of honor for their grand piano, which nestles into a windowed corner by the entry.

THE MASTER SUITE *OPPOSITE* HAS RESTFUL COLORS, A FOUR-POSTER, AND A WINDOW AT THE CEILING PEAK. "IT'S A NICE PLACE TO WAKE UP TO," SAYS BILL. IN THE BATHROOM *LEFT*, A CIRCLEHEAD WINDOW IS SURROUNDED BY A PAINTED SKY.

THE REAR EXTERIOR *BELOW* PRESENTS WALLS OF PELLA® WINDOWS TO THE SOUTHERN SUN.

The dining room, with its elegant black and white stripes and a whitewashed cedar ceiling, is a more relaxed version of formal. It sets the stage for the casual kitchen, where the same cedar covers the walls and ceiling and faces the cabinetry. Bill and Sue were so sure about what they wanted in their kitchen that they planned the lay-out themselves, right down to calculating the dimensions for all the cabinets and appliances.

Upstairs is a world all its own. The home's second level provides a master bed-room, bath, and home office. "We have provided a comfortable and private sitting area in the bedroom," says Bill, "and with Sue's home office adjacent, we have an ideal situation for work and relaxation." In addition, the upstairs has two guest rooms to accommodate visiting family.

"We had a lot to think about in building this house—the lot, the neighborhood, the Conyerses' life-style," says Baldwin. "They wouldn't let me ignore any of their quirks." Bill and Sue think that the time they invested in the design is well worth it. "The longer we live here," says Sue, "the happier we are with it." □

ALL ABOUT WINDOWS AND DOORS

GREAT WINDOWS OF OPPORTUNITY

Each type of window has a personality all its own, and each one has something to say about the architectural style of your home and how the space inside will be used. The Pella® windows shown on these pages are standard products. If your imagination demands more, the Pella Custom Plant (page 65) can build a window to virtually any specification. Select from many available options (pages 70–71) to fit your exact needs.

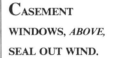

CASEMENT WINDOWS, *ABOVE*, SEAL OUT WIND.

THE BOW WINDOW *ABOVE* IS MADE UP OF CASEMENT WINDOWS SET IN A GRACEFUL CURVE.

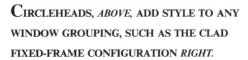

CIRCLEHEADS, *ABOVE*, ADD STYLE TO ANY WINDOW GROUPING, SUCH AS THE CLAD FIXED-FRAME CONFIGURATION *RIGHT*.

VERSATILE AWNING WINDOWS, *LEFT*, MAKE THE MOST OF TIGHT SPACES.

A BAY WINDOW, *ABOVE*, IS AN ELEGANT WAY TO ADD SPACE.

A SUNROOF, *ABOVE*, OPENS YOUR HOME TO SUNSHINE AND BLUE SKIES.

DOUBLE-HUNG WINDOWS WITH WINDOWPANE DIVIDERS, *RIGHT*, ARE CLASSICS.

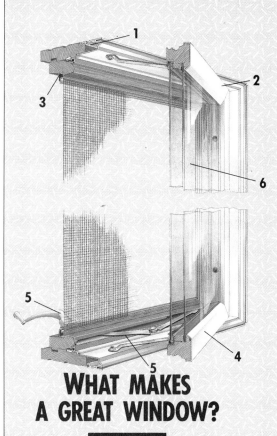

WHAT MAKES A GREAT WINDOW?

1. Wood sashes and frames are best for beauty and insulating capabilities. Pella® windows use kiln-dried western pine, and each piece is treated with water-repellent preservatives that protect against decay and insects.

2. Sash corners are joined with glue, special metal fasteners, and interlocking joints for maximum strength.

3. Continuous welded-at-the-corners weather stripping eliminates drafts. In laboratory testing, Pella Casement windows have been shown to be extremely resistant to air infiltration.

4. Permacoat™ paint finishes are available for aluminum clad windows and doors. This extremely tough coating resists chalking, fading, and corrosion.

5. Hardware is designed for years of trouble-free use.

6. Glazing options include insulating glass, the Double Glazing Panel System, and high-performance glazings that increase energy efficiency.

THE DOORWAYS OF IMAGINATION

Doors always work hard. Every day they open wide, close securely, greet visitors, and guard our homes. A great door does all this, and does it beautifully.

Pella® doors are unsurpassed for style and quality. Each unit is precision built and rigorously tested to ensure lasting integrity. Unique features, such as Warpguard™ laminated construction, and elegant good looks make Pella doors the finest available.

FRENCH SLIDING GLASS DOORS, *LEFT,* **FEATURE BUILT-IN SLIMSHADE® BLINDS.**

TRADITIONAL FRENCH DOORS, *BELOW,* **ARE THE CLASSIC ANSWER TO A CALL FOR ELEGANCE.**

FOLDING DOORS, *BELOW,* **HELP SHAPE AND RESHAPE ROOMS.**

RICHLY CRAFTED WOOD ENTRY DOORS, *LEFT,* **CAN INSPIRE IMAGINATIVE WINDOWSCAPING® DESIGNS.**

SLIDING GLASS DOORS, *RIGHT,* **ARE AMERICAN AS APPLE PIE. THE PELLA® LABEL IS YOUR ASSURANCE OF QUALITY.**

CUSTOM PELLA® PRODUCTS: DREAMS COME TRUE

The Pella® Custom Plant can make practically any window or door system you can imagine—so nothing stands between you and your dreams. Every custom product meets the same high quality standards you've come to expect from the Pella/Rolscreen Company.

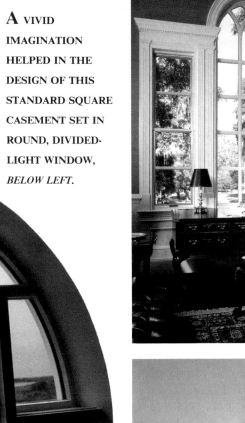

A VIVID IMAGINATION HELPED IN THE DESIGN OF THIS STANDARD SQUARE CASEMENT SET IN ROUND, DIVIDED-LIGHT WINDOW, *BELOW LEFT*.

A CUSTOM ARCH HEAD WINDOW WITH CUSTOM WINDOWPANE DIVIDERS SHOWS TRADITIONAL GRACE AND ELEGANCE WHEN FLANKED BY A PAIR OF STANDARD DOUBLE-HUNG WINDOWS, *LEFT*.

A ROW OF GENTLY CURVED ARCH HEAD WINDOWS, *RIGHT*, BEAUTIFY A BEDROOM.

65

CREATE YOUR OWN VISION OF YOUR WORLD

Few architectural elements are as dazzling and impressive as a cleverly designed arrangement of windows and doors. A wide expanse of glass can create magnificent views, and it opens interiors to the warmth and brilliance of light. The results are dramatic and satisfying—especially when that clever design is your very own.

Putting together a Windowscaping® design is a rewarding experience, and the many standard and custom Pella® products available make the process easy. Begin with a central theme, such as a large circlehead window that opens to a commanding view. Then expand your theme to fill your world with light and to bring the outdoors inside.

BRIGHTEN YOUR OUTLOOK WITH BOLD DESIGNS

Creating a Windowscaping® design is a great opportunity to express your most imaginative ideas. In fact, there's no need to stop at more traditional configurations. With paper and pencil, try your hand at making one-of-a-kind designs that are truly an expression of your individuality.

Your drawings won't have to be perfect, either. Just take your sketches to The Pella Window Store® and talk to the trained professional staff. They'll be able to help refine your ideas, give an estimate of costs, and show you products that can make your dreams come true. A huge selection of standard and custom Pella® products can make almost any design a reality. See page 71 for more information about Pella Window Stores.

A WORLD OF OPTIONS

The many wonderful and imaginative optional features available for all Pella® products will help you enjoy great flexibility and control over your project. Many of these options are designed to work with or without other product features to create *integrated systems.* For example, choose regular, custom, colonial, or traditional windowpane dividers designed to fit inside the innovative Pella Double Glazing Panel System. No matter what optional features you choose, you are assured of getting quality Pella craftsmanship and top performance.

It would be impossible to list all the optional features on these two pages. For complete information, the knowledgeable staff at The Pella Window Store® (see opposite page) can provide answers to all your questions.

FOR THOSE WHO LOVE THE OCEAN, SEACOAST HARDWARE IS ESPECIALLY RESISTANT TO THE CORROSIVE EFFECTS OF SALT MIST AND SPRAY, *BELOW.*

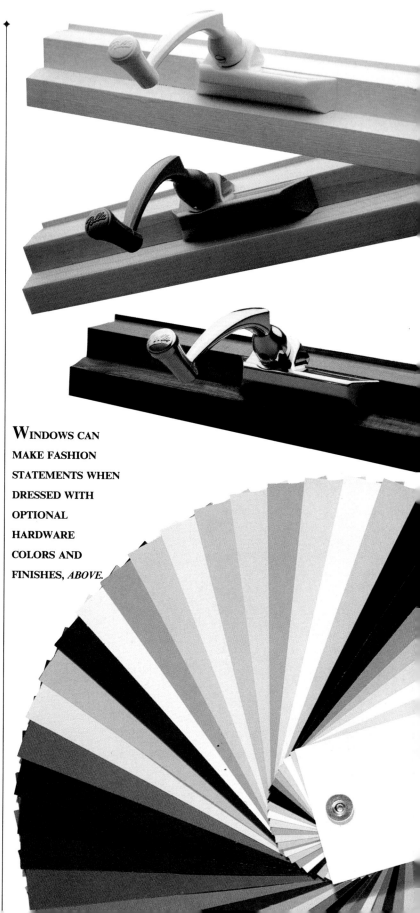

WINDOWS CAN MAKE FASHION STATEMENTS WHEN DRESSED WITH OPTIONAL HARDWARE COLORS AND FINISHES, *ABOVE.*

A GREAT PLACE TO VISIT

It was a Saturday afternoon when Doug and Rhonda Lockin walked into The Pella Window Store® of Des Moines. The Lockins were looking for a replacement door for their family room. What they found was a showroom full of Pella® products—and a whole lot more.

"Our family room is about three feet below the ground," explains Rhonda, "and there's a stairwell to the outside. When it rained we were getting water inside the family room. We thought a new door would help keep the moisture out."

Listening to their problem, a Pella Window Store representative arranged to meet the Lockins at their home. After a careful examination, the representative diagnosed the problems and offered solutions—all free of charge.

"My husband and I aren't very good at seeing the right way to fix things," says Rhonda. "But the person from the Window Store was able to give us some great ideas."

The solution the Lockins liked called for sealing off the old entryway and replacing a kitchen window with a sliding glass door to gain access to the backyard. But it wasn't until Rhonda made another visit to the Pella Window Store that the Lockins decided to put the plan into action.

"On the second trip to the Window Store I saw how Pleated Shades and Slimshade® blinds fit between the glass panes," says Rhonda. "They

won't get dirty and I don't have to clean them. When I saw that, I was sold. It was great to have real live windows and doors right there in the store so you could see how they worked."

The service provided by the Pella Window Store wasn't over yet, however. The Window Store representative then prepared—at no charge—a complete bid for the project that included plumbing, moving a furnace duct, and installing drywall. When the Lockins agreed, the Window Store arranged to have the work completed by a qualified contractor.

"Everyone was very helpful," says Rhonda. "We got personalized service."

And the windows and doors?

"Excellent," she says. "I wouldn't put anything else in my home but Pella products."

THE CONCEPT IS SERVICE

More than 400 Pella Window Stores are located nationwide, each one staffed with trained experts who provide personal assistance—whether it's helping you explore a design idea, demonstrating a product, preparing an estimate, or coordinating a custom order. Window Store professionals represent the creative insights, technical expertise, and extensive experience that stands behind every Pella product. Call your local Pella distributor (see page 128) to find the Window Store nearest you.

71

PLANNING YOUR DREAM

*Y*OU CAN SEE IT IN YOUR MIND'S EYE: THE IDEAL ROOMS, A stunning entryway, the perfect sun-splashed kitchen, a luxurious whirlpool bath beneath a skylight full of stars. Your ideas and goals are clearly defined. Now, use the next section of this book to begin planning your project. You'll find advice and instruction for every phase of the planning project, from hanging towel bars to finding a building contractor and getting financing. Your dreams are closer to reality than ever.

A NEW HOME ON THE HORIZON

Building a new home can be the thrill of a lifetime. It also can be somewhat intimidating. There are hundreds of exciting and difficult decisions to make. With some careful planning, however, you'll be able to make the right choices throughout the process.

One of the first decisions you'll face is where to put your new home. You'll be shopping for a lot that fits your personality and life-style. A wooded lot, for example, surrounds you with privacy and puts nature at your doorstep. An open lot means plenty of sun and views.

Your decision must take into account the quality of the neighborhood, the availability of public services, your proximity to shopping and libraries, and the distance your children will travel to school. Taxes may affect your choice, too. If you don't have children living with you, you may well prefer a community where education is not a large part of the tax budget.

When considering a lot, check to see how much of the property is buildable. Inconveniently placed setbacks, easements, or neighborhood covenants and restrictions may conflict with the type of house you want to build. Find out about the roads, and whether access to your property involves crossing

someone else's. If so, you'll need an easement, or permission to use that land. Your local recorder's office can advise you of easements and setbacks.

Visit the property to get a feel for the land. A steeply sloped lot may offer a grand view, but it might also require a steep driveway that could pose problems in winter. Beware of low-lying areas that could become soaked with moisture in the spring and cause chronic basement flooding. It's possible to have low areas filled, but remember that extensive site preparation work could add as much as 10 percent to the cost of your building project.

When visiting your site, note which direction is south. Check the lot at different times of day to see when your proposed building site is in the sunlight. If possible, you'll want to make sure your home gets its fair share of warming winter sun from the south.

Your next major decision is to select a contractor. Shop around by soliciting names from friends and business associates. Meet with each of the recommended builders. A preliminary chat can give you a strong idea of your ability to communicate easily with each candidate—an important consideration. Make certain each is bonded, insured, and carries worker's compensation insurance; otherwise, you could be liable for any accident that happens on your property. Check out other projects the builder has completed to observe the

BUILDING A NEW HOME IS EXCITING AND CHALLENGING. MAKE SURE YOUR GOALS ARE MET BY EXAMINING THE BUILDING SITE, CAREFULLY SHOPPING FOR A BUILDING CONTRACTOR, AND GETTING ALL DETAILS AND SPECIFICATIONS FOR THE PROJECT IN A WRITTEN CONTRACT.

Photograph: William D. Adams/ SuperStock

quality of workmanship. Finally, ask the candidates for written bids based on the exact same set of plans. Check each bid for its thoroughness and attention to detail. For example, an acceptable bid should mention a complete cleanup of the building site. Make your final selection based not only on the quoted price but also on the workmanship you have observed and your ability to communicate with the builder clearly and effectively.

BREAKING THE GROUND

Once a contractor has earned your confidence and you have secured financing for your project (see pages 82–83), put your deal on paper. A good contract spells out in detail each part of a job, and the wording should be clear to the homeowner. The contract should cover starting and completion dates; lists of materials (called *schedules*); a guarantee covering the work for a minimum of three years; a method of payment. When the job is completed, conduct a thorough inspection. Draw up a list of anything that needs attending to and schedule definite dates for repairs.

T*he best thing you can bring to an initial meeting with a builder is a realistic idea of what you want to spend. . . . Also, it wouldn't hurt to check on local zoning and building codes to make sure you can build the type of house you want on the site.*

—**Greg Hunt**
General contractor, Phoenix

ADVICE FROM A PROFESSIONAL BUILDER

Greg Hunt, of Phoenix, Arizona, is a Certified Pella® Contractor. His company, G.M. Hunt Building and Remodeling, Inc., has been constructing new homes and taking on major remodelings in Phoenix for more than eight years.

Q. How can a client look into a builder's reputation?

A. References and word of mouth are two ways. You can also check with Pella distributors for a list of their certified contractors. A Pella representative can also refer you to quality contractors in your area.

Q. What are the benefits of using a Certified Pella Contractor?

A. You're assured of a quality installation, for one thing. And if any problems do arise, they will be attended to without delay.

Q. Does a builder always serve as a general contractor, coordinating the work done by carpenters, electricians, plumbers, and others, or can this be handled by the homeowner?

A. It can be handled by the homeowner, but in my experience, this has never worked out to their satisfaction. The delegating of responsibility takes tremendous amounts of time and can be very frustrating. I wouldn't recommend it.

Q. When visiting a builder's job sites, what marks of quality should clients look for?

A. The cleanliness of a job site is especially important. A clean job is an efficient job. But there are signs of quality in the framing or roofing stages that should be pointed out to a potential client. The best thing to do is walk through the site with the builder so he can explain exactly why he's done things the way he has.

Q. What specific preparations should a person make before talking to a builder?

A. The best thing you can bring to an initial meeting with a builder is a realistic idea of what you want to spend. This is absolutely critical. Also, how soon do you want to be in the house? Also, it wouldn't hurt to check on local zoning and building codes to make sure you can build the type of house you want on the site.

Q. Should the builder and client be personally compatible?

A. It's never been a problem for me, but on a 1 to 10 scale, it's about an 8 in importance. Building a house should be a good experience for both parties. It's important that you get along.

Q. What features do clients ask for in today's new homes, features that might help sell the home later on?

A. My clients want a large, luxurious master bath and master bedroom, as well as the latest in kitchen appliances. They want lots of windows and light. Entertainment rooms are popular too. All of this has been pretty consistent in recent years. I haven't noticed any downscaling of these areas. Houses themselves are getting bigger, if anything.

Q. What percentage of the total house cost is the builder's fee?

A. Ten to 15 percent, on average.

Q. What services should the client expect the builder to provide after the house is built?

A. Most builders will stand behind their work. I'll do a number of on-site inspections and go back to the house several times to take care of odds and ends or anything the homeowner has had a problem with.

I also handle all the guarantees of the subcontractors so the homeowner just has to deal with one person. I'll also do a thorough inspection one year after completion.

STYLE		1,000	1,200	1,400	1,600	1,800	2,000	2,400	2,800	3,200	3,600	4,000
		SIZE IN SQUARE FEET										
1-Story	Luxury	$99,000	$109,980	$120,680	$130,480	$142,200	$154,200	$172,800	$190,680	$210,240	$224,640	$242,200
	Average	62,200	69,420	76,160	82,640	90,450	98,400	110,280	121,520	134,240	n/a	n/a
	Economy	49,700	55,260	60,340	65,120	71,190	77,400	86,160	94,360	104,000	n/a	n/a
1½-Story	Luxury	$92,850	$103,200	$114,100	$123,840	$134,100	$142,500	$155,640	$175,000	$193,280	$210,240	$221,400
	Average	62,700	70,320	78,400	85,440	93,060	99,300	108,720	122,920	136,480	n/a	n/a
	Economy	50,450	56,340	62,720	68,080	73,980	78,800	85,440	96,460	106,720	n/a	n/a
2-Story	Luxury	n/a	$105,180	$116,200	$127,520	$137,520	$146,100	$163,080	$179,340	$193,920	$211,140	$229,800
	Average	67,300	72,600	80,780	89,280	96,750	103,100	116,275	126,865	138,120	n/a	n/a
	Economy	54,950	59,160	65,660	72,480	78,480	83,300	93,590	101,705	110,385	120,505	n/a
Split-Level	Luxury	n/a	$98,400	$108,780	$119,360	$128,790	$136,900	$153,120	$168,560	$182,720	$199,080	$216,800
	Average	62,150	66,960	74,620	82,560	89,640	95,500	107,945	118,225	129,010	141,380	n/a
	Economy	50,500	54,240	60,270	66,560	72,270	76,700	83,785	94,185	102,470	112,050	n/a

THE TABLE *LEFT* SHOWS TYPICAL BUILDING COSTS FOR LUXURY, AVERAGE, AND ECONOMY HOMES BASED ON STYLE AND SIZE. COSTS ARE FOR A WOOD-FRAME HOUSE WITH WOOD SIDING. TO ADJUST THESE COSTS TO YOUR LOCALE, LOCATE THE SYMBOL AND NUMBER THAT CORRESPONDS TO YOUR AREA ON THE MAP. MULTIPLY THAT NUMBER BY THE TYPICAL BUILDING COST OF YOUR STYLE OF HOME.

.84 ▲
.89 ■
.94 ●
.98 ✦
.99 ❖
1.02 ✚
1.16 ♠
1.21 ★
1.26 ◉

GETTING READY TO REMODEL

Once you've decided to remodel and have planned your project, you are ready to select a contractor. Your goals should be to find a qualified firm, determine a fair price, and negotiate a contract that will keep your project running smoothly.

CHOOSING A CONTRACTOR

Most large-scale remodelings require the services of a general contracting firm. A general contractor manages your project from start to finish, including hiring, scheduling, and paying subcontractors who will work on your home. For small projects such as adding a deck or replacing windows, you may get a better value by hiring a tradesperson or a specialty contractor.

Start your search for a contractor by getting recommendations from friends or architects you may know. You can also contact the The Pella Window Store® for a list of Certified Pella Contractors—builders who are specially trained in the installation of Pella products. Once you've identified four or five candidates, begin a selection process.

■ **Meet with each firm.** Discuss the size, scope, and features of your project, and ask about the firm's background and qualifications. Years of experience, an office location, and membership in a national remodeling organization are all good indicators of professionalism. Request written proof that the company carries insurance for property damage, liability, and worker's compensation.

■ **Check references for each firm.** Call past clients to see if the firm completes its jobs on time, on budget, and in a satisfactory manner. Personally visit one or more completed jobs. (The interview on page 80 tells you what to look for.) Also check the firm's track record with the Better Business Bureau, and contact the company's banker to see if the firm is financially sound.

■ **Solicit bids from at least three companies you consider fully qualified for the job.** Request a single, fixed-price bid that represents your total out-of-pocket cost, including labor, materials, fees, and taxes. Ask each firm to bid on identical plans and specifications so that you can fairly compare prices.

■ **Evaluate bids based on overall value.** The lowest price isn't always the best deal. A bargain-basement bid may mean that the contractor is substituting inferior materials or omitting some costs, such as cleanup. If bids vary widely, ask for a breakdown of labor and material costs.

Base your final choice on a mix of quality, price, and your comfort with the firm. You can use the winning bid as the basis for obtaining financing for your project. Pages 82–83 tell you how to find the money you need.

WRITING THE CONTRACT

Even for small jobs, insist on a written contract. The contract should give a complete description of all work to be performed, subcontractors to be hired, and materials to be used, right down to the brand name and model number of appliances, windows, and other products. State that the work will be done "in a workmanlike manner"—which means correctly.

Your contract should also cover price. Usually it's in your interest to state a single fixed price. In some cases, however, you may benefit from a "cost-plus" contract. With cost-plus pricing, you agree to pay all labor and material—plus a contractor's fee—up to a guaranteed maximum. This type of pricing makes sense if you want to encourage workers to do a meticulous job, or if you plan to help with construction in order to hold down costs. If you own a very old home, where hidden problems are likely, contractors may insist on a cost-plus contract.

A sound contract also:
■ states the approximate calendar dates for start and completion of work, with flexibility for weather-related delays;
■ sets out the payment schedule and any fees that apply if you cancel the project;
■ outlines procedures to follow if you want to amend your plans;
■ describes warranties that apply and means of settling disputes;
■ stipulates that the contractor must obtain permits, comply with building codes, and carry insurance;
■ includes a release of liens so that a subcontractor can't slap a lien on your property as a result of a dispute with the general contractor.

NEW WINDOWS TAKE THEIR PLACE IN A LIVING ROOM REMODELING. TO GET TOP PERFORMANCE FROM YOUR PELLA® WINDOWS AND DOORS, CHOOSE A CERTIFIED PELLA CONTRACTOR—A FIRM THAT IS SPECIALLY TRAINED IN INSTALLING PELLA PRODUCTS.

TALKING WITH A REMODELING CONTRACTOR

The CPC program involves ongoing education that keeps a contractor qualified for the correct installation of Pella products. As a company, we don't sell jobs, we sell service. Pella/Rolscreen is the same way.

—**Mark Brick**
Remodeling Contractor, Milwaukee

Mark Brick started B & E General Contractors, Milwaukee, in 1985 with two employees. Some 600 remodelings later, he now manages 15 employees who handle everything from window replacements to five-figure remodelings. Mark says he has built his business on service, citing the fact that most of his current jobs are referrals.

Q. You're a Certified Pella® Contractor (CPC). What does that mean for your clients?

A. The CPC program involves ongoing education that keeps a contractor qualified for correct installation of Pella products. We know the product, so the windows are installed correctly, and we're trained to handle any problems that may arise down the line. As a company, we don't sell jobs, we sell service. Pella/Rolscreen is the same way.

Q. How can a person check on the quality of a remodeler's work?

A. Naturally, past references are important. Talk to people the contractor has worked for and try to see the work. Look at the joints and mitering to make sure everything matches and lines up. See if the drywall surface is even or streaking. When it all looks tied together, it's usually done right. If the work is intended to match what exists already, make sure that it does. You can also check with the National Association of the Remodeling Industry, the Remodelors Council, or the National Kitchen and Bath Association to see if the company is a member.

Q. Do most homeowners know what they want in a remodeling?

A. Not always. They may want to add a great-room, but that's not a very defined concept. So you have to help create ideas, based on the client's lifestyle, then design working plans accordingly. Every situation is unique.

Q. What will it cost to develop plans?

A. Plans can cost from 3 to 6 percent of the total cost of the job. We incorporate this fee into the project price if the client decides to go ahead with it.

Q. What is specified in your written contracts with a client?

A. Contracts are very specific about everything, from materials to labor. We spell out what will be done beginning with demolition, then going into excavation, plans and permits, masonry, framing, exteriors, roofing, electricity and plumbing, drywall, and finished carpentry. Everything is covered.

Q. Are there ever unforeseen costs?

A. Usually the only cost overruns occur when people want to change something while the job is under way.

Also, we might be digging for a crawl space and find the ground isn't stable—usually in landfill areas. But this might only happen in one out of a hundred jobs.

Q. Do you recommend that homeowners considering major remodeling get an appraisal?

A. Definitely. And on the upscale projects, a bank will insist on it. They'll want to see the plans and get an idea of what the property will be worth when the job is finished.

Q. Have you ever told homeowners that their proposed remodeling might cost more than their location can justify?

A. Yes, generally based on their neighborhood. In such cases I'll suggest that they get a second opinion or check with a real estate professional. I'll also sit down with them and try to find out why they're doing the remodeling. If they're doing it solely to suit their family's lifestyle, I'll try to give them as much as we can for their money.

Q. If the appraisal shows that they probably won't be able to get their money back, have you ever told the homeowners that they shouldn't remodel?

A. Yes, I've told clients it might be better to buy or build a new home when they've priced themselves out of the area. But I can also present them with alternatives by downscaling the proposed project a bit.

LABOR, OVERHEAD, AND PROFIT MAKE UP MORE THAN 60 PERCENT OF THE COST OF A PROFESSIONAL REMODELING, SAYS A 1989 SURVEY OF CONTRACTORS. TO CONTROL COSTS, BID YOUR PROJECT, CHOOSE A SKILLED FIRM, AND STICK TO YOUR PLANS.

USE THE TABLE *RIGHT* TO GET AN IDEA OF WHAT YOUR REMODELING MIGHT COST. FOR EXAMPLE, A SIMPLE 10×10-FOOT DECK MAY RUN $2,000—100 SQUARE FEET AT $20 EACH. ACTUAL COSTS VARY WITH LOCAL LABOR COSTS AND THE SPECIFICS OF YOUR PROJECT.

RESIDENTIAL REMODELING: WHERE YOUR MONEY GOES

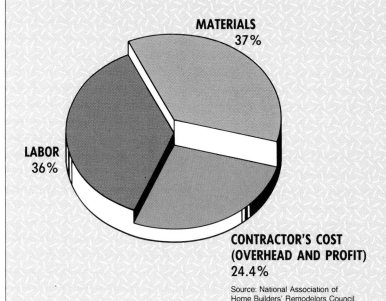

MATERIALS 37%

LABOR 36%

CONTRACTOR'S COST (OVERHEAD AND PROFIT) 24.4%

Source: National Association of Home Builders' Remodelors Council

REMODELING COSTS
(Per square foot)

Standard L-shape kitchen	$82
Premium L-shape kitchen	$123
Regular U-shape kitchen	$96
Premium U-shape kitchen	$150
Regular half-bath	$92
Premium half-bath	$130
Regular master bath	$85
Premium master bath	$115
Garage conversion, no plumbing	$22
Simple deck	$20
Complex redwood deck	$32
Attic conversion, no plumbing	$25
Basement conversion, no plumbing	$16
Walk-out basement	$32
Entryway addition	$104
Family room addition	$68
Second-story addition	$83

FINANCING YOUR DREAM

There's one kind of building material that's required of any size project—money. How much money you are going to spend can determine the size and scope of your project, as well as the quality of the construction team you assemble to complete the work. Obviously, you'll want to protect your investment with financial planning as carefully thought out as any blueprint.

MONEY FOR REMODELING

Remodeling your home may cost a few hundred dollars—or tens of thousands. The range of possibilities makes remodeling a popular pastime, and creates a number of ways to finance your project. Your search for cash should always include a careful comparison of interest rates from several possible sources. You'll want to be sure you're making the best financial decisions.

■ Your personal accounts are a primary source. Money held in savings or checking accounts may cover the costs entirely or help lower the amount you would have to borrow from another source, such as a bank. The best guideline is to compare interest rates. If your savings or other accounts are earning a higher interest rate than you

are charged from a lender, it's probably a good idea to borrow the entire amount from the lender. Remember also that some long-term savings plans have penalties for early withdrawals.

■ Credit cards or life insurance loans are another personal resource. Credit cards may be able to finance part or all of your project. In essence, you are taking a loan that's already been approved up to the limit of your credit. You also may be able to borrow from your life insurance policy—up to 95 percent of its cash value depending on the type of policy.

■ You may be able to qualify

for a conventional loan from a bank, credit union, or other lending institution. Depending on the size and cost of the project, as well as your credit history, you should be able to get a conventional loan, and many lenders have special rates for home improvement loans. To qualify, a loan officer may ask that you submit detailed plans of your project for inspection. Other sources of conventional loans include savings and loan associations, mortgage companies, and finance offices.

■ A home-equity loan allows you to borrow against the money you've already invested in your home—including down payment and principal. Usually a home-equity loan requires refinancing your home

mortgage or taking out a second mortgage, and offering your house as collateral. Refinancing may mean lowering the interest rate you'll pay, but there will be closing costs involved. The rule of thumb is that the new interest rate should be at least 2 points below your current rate to make refinancing worthwhile. Rates for second mortgages may be several points higher than your current mortgage.

FINANCING YOUR NEW HOME

There's no standard way to finance a new home. However, it's in your best interest to spend some time shopping around for your mortgage. For help with your search, look in the yellow pages under Mortgages for mortgage brokers,

who specialize in matching borrowers with lenders. Shop by comparing interest rates and terms from a variety of lending institutions. Check appraisal fees, legal costs, points, prepayment penalties, and title insurance fees. In all instances you should proceed carefully and make sure all your questions are answered to your satisfaction.

Lenders offer many kinds of mortgage options. Conventional fixed-rate loans represent only one of many possible strategies.

■ Adjustable-rate mortgages, called ARMs, have changeable interest rates that move up and down according to market trends. This type of mortgage usually has attractive initial rates that are below current market rates. There is a risk that rising rates may cause your payments to increase.

■ Convertible mortgages allow you to switch from an adjustable to a fixed rate after a predetermined amount of time has passed. This type of mortgage can be especially convenient if interest rates should start to rise.

■ Graduated payment mortgages have monthly payments that increase over time. A graduated payment mortgage may work if initial rates are attractively low and you are confident that your income will rise.

■ Deferred interest mortgages have low initial rates and switch to higher rates at some predetermined point in the future. If you sell your house you'll pay all the interest that's been deferred.

■ Flexible-payment mortgages have initial payments that are interest only; later, the mortgage is amortized and payments increase. □

THE LOAN ARRANGER
YOUR GUIDE TO AFFORDABILITY

Monthly Payment	7.00%	7.50%	8.00%	8.50%	9.00%	9.50%	10.00%	10.50%	11.00%	12.00%	13.00%
$ 300	45,092	42,905	40,885	39,016	37,285	35,678	34,185	32,796	31,502	29,166	27,120
$ 350	52,608	50,056	47,699	45,519	43,499	41,624	39,883	38,262	36,752	34,026	31,640
$ 400	60,123	57,207	54,513	52,022	49,713	47,571	45,580	43,728	42,003	38,887	36,160
$ 450	67,638	64,358	61,438	58,524	55,927	53,517	51,278	49,194	47,253	43,748	40,680
$ 500	75,154	71,509	68,142	65,027	62,141	59,463	56,975	54,660	52,503	48,609	45,200
$ 550	82,669	78,660	74,956	71,529	68,355	65,410	62,673	60,126	57,753	53,470	49,720
$ 600	90,185	85,811	81,770	78,032	74,569	71,356	68,370	65,592	63,004	58,331	54,240
$ 650	97,700	92,961	88,584	84,535	80,783	77,302	74,068	71,059	68,254	63,192	58,760
$ 700	105,215	100,112	95,398	91,038	86,997	83,249	79,766	76,525	73,504	68,053	63,280
$ 750	112,731	107,263	102,213	97,540	93,211	89,195	85,463	81,991	78,755	72,914	67,800
$ 800	120,246	114,414	109,027	104,043	99,425	95,141	91,161	87,457	84,005	77,775	72,320
$ 850	127,761	121,565	115,841	110,546	105,640	101,088	96,858	92,923	89,255	82,636	76,840
$ 900	135,277	128,716	122,655	117,048	111,854	107,034	102,556	98,389	94,506	87,497	81,360
$ 950	142,792	135,867	129,469	123,551	118,068	112,980	108,253	103,854	99,756	92,357	85,880
$1,000	150,308	143,018	136,283	130,054	124,282	118,927	113,951	109,321	105,006	97,218	90,400
$1,050	157,823	150,169	143,098	136,556	130,496	124,873	119,648	114,786	110,156	102,079	94,920
$1,100	165,338	157,320	149,912	143,058	136,710	130,820	125,340	120,252	115,506	106,940	99,440
$1,150	172,854	164,471	156,726	149,561	142,924	136,766	131,043	125,718	120,757	111,801	103,960
$1,200	180,369	171,621	163,540	156,064	149,138	142,712	136,741	131,185	126,007	116,662	108,480
$1,250	187,884	178,772	170,354	162,567	155,352	148,659	142,439	136,651	131,257	121,523	113,000

To DETERMINE THE MORTGAGE AMOUNT YOU CAN AFFORD, FIRST ESTIMATE YOUR MONTHLY PAYMENT. THEN READ ACROSS TO THE CLOSEST CURRENT INTEREST RATE. THE AMOUNTS LISTED ARE FOR MORTGAGES BASED ON A 30-YEAR FIXED-RATE LOAN, AND INCLUDE ONLY PRINCIPAL AND INTEREST.

COOKING UP TERRIFIC KITCHENS

The kitchen can be the most livable room in your home. It is the place where the family naturally gathers and where guests are often most at ease. A kitchen should be a relaxed haven that invites sunny dispositions and makes meal preparation a pleasure. Good planning will ensure that this important room fulfills the needs of you and your family.

THE WORK TRIANGLE

In the 1950s, a Cornell University study determined that in order to maximize efficiency and reduce unnecessary steps, a kitchen should be divided into three main centers of work: the refrigerator, the sink, and the range. A line was drawn from the refrigerator to the sink, to the cooking surface, and then back to the refrigerator. According to the study, the perimeter of the "triangle" created should total no more than 22 feet, nor should it be less than 12 feet. Each leg of the triangle should be between 4 and 7 feet long.

To be effective, the triangle should not be interrupted by traffic, and cabinetry should not intersect any of the triangle legs. For the last four decades, the classic work triangle has proved to be an effective design tool. Many designers, however, believe that the work triangle concept should be expanded to accommodate the ways we use our kitchens today.

Adding a microwave oven or a second sink or cooktop, for example, creates a rectangle, a pentagon, or even a second triangle. This expansion of the triangle enables homeowners to plan a space designed to meet their family's needs. For example, a cook who works full-time outside the home is likely to make extensive use of the microwave to speed up meal preparation. This appliance, then, should be included as a fourth point in the work area. Kitchens with duplicate work areas are ideal for accommodating two or more cooks.

COMFORT AND CONVENIENCE

The work triangle determines the amount and shape of the floor space needed in a kitchen, but a well-planned kitchen must also consider comfort, storage space, and sources of light.

■ **Build the cabinets to fit the cook(s).** The Comfort Zones chart on *page 86* was developed for individuals ranging in height from 5 feet, 3 inches to 5 feet, 7 inches. If your cook is taller or shorter, you may want to adjust the suggested distances. If you customize, be aware that going beyond these standards by too much may adversely affect the resale value of your home.

♦ **THE TRIANGULAR ISLAND IN THIS KITCHEN HOSTS TWO WORK CENTERS: ONE AT THE SIX-BURNER COOKTOP, AND ANOTHER AT THE ROUND VEGETABLE SINK. PELLA® WINDOWS AND SKYLIGHTS FORM A TRIANGULAR BUMP-OUT THAT'S HOME TO TWO CIRCULAR SINKS AND TWO DISHWASHERS. THE LIGHT-FILLED CORNER MAKES CLEANUP MUCH LESS OF A CHORE.**

CABINET CRITERIA

Standard base cabinet height	34½ inches
Standard counter height	36 inches
Maximum counter height	38 inches
Minimum counter height	30 inches
Recommended mixing counter height	32 inches
Standard counter extension beyond base cabinets	1¾ inches
Toe space minimum	3 inches high, 4 inches deep
Distance between counter and upper cabinets	15 to 18 inches
Wall cabinet height	33 to 42 inches
Space required for base cabinets to turn a corner	27 inches on both walls
Space requirements for upper cabinets to turn a corner	15 inches on both walls
Total shelf area	Not less than 50 square feet with not less than 20 square feet in either wall or base cabinet
Total countertop area	Not less than 11 square feet: 4 lineal feet at each work area except sink; 8 feet at sink
Total drawer area	11 square feet minimum
Backsplash	4-inch minimum

COMFORT ZONES

Lowest comfortable reach	2 feet above floor
Highest comfortable reach over a counter	68 inches from floor
Highest comfortable reach without counter	77 inches from floor
It's difficult to see items on a shelf higher than	61 inches
Store items that are used daily no higher than	74 inches
Aisle space minimum	3 feet, 4 feet opposite work areas, 4½ feet if two cook
Aisle space maximum	6 feet

CORRIDOR   ISLAND   U-SHAPE

The work triangle, as indicated by the shaded triangles in the floor plans *above*, connects the kitchen's cooktop or range, refrigerator, and sink. These three areas define the three primary work centers of a kitchen.

■ **A place for everything.** A good kitchen design stores utensils, small appliances, and pots and pans near where these items will be used. Make sure there are enough shelves to fit all the supplies you like to keep on hand. Special items—a set of heirloom bowls from Grandmother, or an unusual appliance such as a pasta maker—should have their own storage area. The Cabinet Criteria chart *left* includes the standard space allotments for cabinetry, and provides minimums for shelf, drawer, and countertop area.

■ **The enlightened kitchen.** Today's kitchens are bright and inviting. Plan plenty of windows to make this special room a pleasure to work in. If wall space is at a premium, skylights can add sun without sacrificing cabinet storage. Built-in kitchen eating areas provide the ideal place to install glass doors to your backyard deck or patio.

SHAPING UP YOUR KITCHEN

The most efficient floor plans provide room for family members and guests yet organize activities according to carefully defined traffic patterns and task areas.

■ **U-shape.** The U-shape kitchen's dead-end design prevents the kitchen from becoming a household traffic artery. This practical kitchen shape, *below left,* also provides three walls of storage and counter space. You'll need kitchen walls at least 8 feet apart to provide a minimum 4 feet of working room in the center of the U. Keep in mind that the perimeter of the work triangle should be no greater than 22 feet.

■ **L-shape.** The two adjacent walls in an L-shape kitchen layout form a natural triangle that protects the cook from interference. If the work area is kept close to the corner of the L, household traffic can flow by without crossing through the triangle. The plan offers flexibility in the arrangement of appliances, storage, and counter space. The work itself should flow from refrigerator to sink to cooking and serving areas. If you switch the order of the work centers, you could create more steps for yourself, making the plan less efficient.

If you are remodeling, keep in mind that the L-shape kitchen requires less space than the U-shape layout and can be almost as efficient.

■ **Corridor.** Although kitchen designers try to keep traffic from crossing through the work triangle, that's impossible to do with a corridor floor plan, shown *opposite below, far left.* Closing off one

doorway can solve the problem, but be sure to plan an alternate route for traffic. The best work-center arrangement for a galley kitchen places the refrigerator and the sink on one wall and the range on the opposite wall. The aisle between counters should measure no less than 4 feet and no more than 6 feet.

■ **Island.** An island in a kitchen can shorten the distance between work centers and direct traffic outside the work triangle. Quite popular in today's kitchens, the island works well in U-shape kitchens with more than 10 feet between the legs of the U, and also in L-shape kitchens. Islands are especially useful in minimizing the work triangle in a large kitchen. Islands usually house either the cleanup center or the cooking center. Designing one side of the island as a counter dining spot alleviates the

need for a separate kitchen eating area.

■ **Peninsula.** This floor plan doesn't require as much room as an island plan. It is the perfect solution for kitchens that have floor space available but have run out of wall space. Peninsulas also work well in kitchens that are open to nearby dining or family areas; they divert traffic around the work area. If the peninsula provides space for a major appliance, it can reduce the size of a too-large work triangle. Although a peninsula can be scaled to fit many floor plans, it may not work in a very small kitchen.

■ **One-of-a-kind kitchen layouts.** Many variations of floor plans are possible. A kitchen that breaks the mold can be as efficient as any of the standard plans discussed previously. Whatever layout you select, remember that the kitchen should have an *uninterrupted* work triangle with a perimeter that measures between 12 and 22 feet.

THE PRIMARY WORK CENTERS

After you've determined the layout, you need to plan the individual work centers. As defined by the work triangle, each kitchen should be divided into at least three activity areas: food storage and preparation, cooking, and cleanup.

■ **Food storage and preparation.** The key to designing an efficient food storage and preparation center, such as the one shown *left,* is to design it with your own personal cooking style in mind.

What kind of foods do you prepare most often, prepackaged or from scratch? Cooking after 5 p.m. may require a center designed for warm-and-serve convenience. Weekends, however, may be spent cooking meals to warm up later, or, perhaps, creating those culinary delights that there just isn't time to make on weeknights. When you do cook, which small appliances do you use most frequently: the food processor, electric mixer, or an electric knife? You need a minimum of 36 inches of counter space to store small appliances and canisters of your most-used ingredients.

The handiest location for the food preparation area is between the cooking center and sink. Foods often require rinsing, and many foods are transferred from the food preparation area directly to the cooktop, microwave, or conventional oven. Placing the refrigerator and a pantry near the preparation area adds convenience. *Cabinet storage.* The most sensible cabinets for storing food items that don't require refrigeration are those attached to cool outside walls, near shaded or west- and north-facing windows. Cabinets near heat sources—including the dishwasher, oven, refrigerator, and southern exterior walls—are not the best choice for foods. For more information on cabinets, see the chart on *page 86. Refrigerator storage.* How much food do you refrigerate? How much do you freeze? Depending on your family's size

and life-style, you may need to increase or decrease the amount of space needed. For a general estimate of your cool-storage capacity requirements, use the formula shown in the chart on *page 91. Refrigerator location.* The refrigerator should be placed where you unload groceries and where the door can swing completely open so bins can be pulled out for cleaning or loading. For added convenience, the refrigerator should open away from the work triangle. At least 15 inches of counter space is needed next to the refrigerator's handle side. To increase floor space, consider a refrigerator that is only 24 inches deep instead of the standard 30- or 33-inch-deep unit.

■ **Cooking.** The cooking center includes the cooktop or range; the microwave oven; storage for pans, utensils, and hot pads; and space for foods that go directly from container to simmering pot. The cooktop is most efficient, and safest, if at least 18 inches of counter space is open on both sides, as shown *below.* This enables you to turn pan handles away

EFFERVESCENT WITH COLORS FROM NATURE, THE KITCHEN *RIGHT* COAXES YOU TO COME IN AND LINGER. AN ANTIQUE BUTCHER BLOCK DOUBLES AS AN ISLAND FOR FOOD PREPARATION.

THE COOKTOP SHOWN *BELOW* IS ONLY TWO STEPS BEHIND THE ANTIQUE ISLAND SHOWN AT *RIGHT,* MAKING IT EASY TO TRANSFER FOODS.

from the front of the cooktop, and provides room for setting down hot pots after removing them from the heat.

In today's kitchens, the conventional oven, *when separate from the cooktop*, is the least used of the major appliances, and may be placed outside of the kitchen work triangle. However, if your built-in oven includes a microwave, this recommendation is inappropriate. The microwave, a frequently used appliance, should be placed within the most active portion of the kitchen. See the chart *opposite* for additional recommendations. **Note:** Although popular, commercial cooking equipment is *not* recommended for most kitchens because of specific power requirements, ventilation needs, and cookware restrictions. If you like the commercial look, select a brand that offers a similar appearance but is still designed for residential use.

■ **Cleanup center.** Cleanup activities center around the sink, garbage disposal, and dishwasher. For optimum efficiency, the cleanup center should be placed between the food preparation and cooking centers. Plan for 30 to 36 inches of counter space on both sides of the sink. For more cleanup center dimensions, see the chart *opposite*.

The dishwasher should be placed to the left of the sink if you are right-handed, to the right of the sink if you are left-handed. How you use your dishwasher and whether or not you use a disposal may dictate your selection of sinks. Double sinks, such as the one shown in the photograph *right,* are usually the sink of choice. However, a compartmentalized sink is an excellent alternative if space is a consideration.

An array of faucets and fittings is available for sinks, including special

dispensers for purified drinking and hot water. Be sure everyone in your house is familiar with the dispensers you choose: A hot-water dispenser should be used with caution.

Whether you choose to store everyday dishes and silverware near the dishwasher or at the serving center, plan for ample cabinet storage.

SECONDARY WORK CENTERS

Besides food storage, cooking, and cleanup, plan secondary work centers for specialized activities such as baking, dining, planning, and recycling. Reviewing your family's life-style will

THE SMALL PELLA® SUNROOM *BELOW* PROVIDES A SPOT FOR AN INDOOR GARDEN AND PROVIDES A VIEW OF THE GREAT OUTDOORS FOR THE PERSON IN CHARGE OF CLEANUP.

help you tailor these activity centers to meet the individual needs of your family. Be careful not to overload your kitchen—if it's a family room and a dining room, maybe it shouldn't be an office too.

■ **Dining center.** With today's busy lifestyles, more and more families choose to eat their weekday meals in the kitchen instead of the dining room. The number of people you feed at one time determines how much room you'll need for this activity.

If your space is limited, consider a bar attached to the kitchen work surface. If you prefer more of a separation, consider a banquette; it requires less area than a freestanding table and chairs. However, banquettes are less convenient for serving and eating. The chart at *right* provides the dimensions required for dining in the kitchen.

■ **Baking center.** If baking is one of your hobbies, you'll appreciate the convenience of a baking center. The ideal location is between the oven and refrigerator. A counter at least 36 inches long, 30 inches wide, and 3 to 6 inches lower than the standard 36-inch countertop is comfortable for kneading and rolling out dough. Shadow-free lighting and a heat-resistant surface (a marble or granite insert is the best choice for rolling out doughs) are also needed. Plan storage for cookbooks, mixing bowls, baking utensils, baking pans, small appliances (appliance garages are ideal), and for staples such as flour, sugar, and spices.

■ **Planning center.** Any kitchen with a few extra feet of floor space can benefit from a small office area. It's best to locate the planning center away from the main work area.

You'll need to provide adequate lighting for paperwork, storage for supplies, a calendar for keeping track of the family's activities, and a phone. The minimum dimensions required for a kitchen planning center are shown in the chart *right*.

■ **Recycling center.** Every year, more cities and towns are requiring garbage to be sorted prior to pickup. To organize this task, install a recycling drawer that has room for three or four plastic containers—each large enough to hold a standard brown paper bag—for glass, paper, plastic, or cans. If your home has a basement or lower-level garage, consider installing separate chutes that lead directly to receptacles located on the lower level.

■ **Family room.** If a combination kitchen and social area is your goal, consider a peninsula or island kitchen. These kitchens provide a natural transition between the social and work areas. To the kitchen side, they provide a work surface. To the social side, they offer guests a spot to pull up and talk with the cook. For more definition between the two areas, use overhead cabinets to physically divide the space, and/or consider changing ceiling heights and floor levels. Skylights can also be used to visually separate the two spaces.

LIGHTING'S ROLE

Proper lighting plays a major part in successful kitchen design. Dark interiors are a thing of the past. Bright, open spaces provide a much more welcome, cheery atmosphere. Task lighting focuses on a specific work area, preventing eyestrain. Accent lighting spotlights collections and decorative items.

WORK CENTER STANDARDS

The chart *below* provides the standard dimensions for five of the most common activity centers: storage, cooking, cleanup, dining, and planning.

COOL STORAGE

■ **Refrigerator/freezer capacity**—Plan 12 cubic feet for 2 people; add 2 cubic feet for each additional person.

■ **Refrigerator/freezer dimensions**—Refrigerators with top freezer are 28 to 30 inches wide. Side-by-side refrigerators are 30 to 36 inches wide. Depths vary from 24 to 33 inches.

COOKING CENTER

■ **Counter clearance beside range/cooktop**—Plan 18 to 24 inches on each side.

■ **Counter clearance beside island cooktop**—Plan at least 12 inches on each side.

■ **Microwave clearance**—Plan an area 14 to 18 inches in depth and 20 to 24 inches in width.

CLEANUP CENTER

■ **Double sink**—Requires 36-inch base cabinet.

■ **Single sink**—Requires 30-inch base cabinet.

■ **Dishwasher width**—The standard width is 24 inches. The compact width is 18 inches.

■ **Counter clearance beside sink**—On the dishwasher side, plan 24 to 36 inches. On the other side, plan 18 to 36 inches.

■ **Trash compactor width**—There are three standard widths, 12, 15, and 18 inches.

DINING AND PLANNING CENTER

■ **Standard counter height**—36 inches; requires a stool that is 24 inches high.

■ **Standard table height**—30 inches; requires a standard chair that is 18 inches high.

■ **Bar height standard**—42 inches; requires a stool that is 30 to 32 inches high.

■ **Minimum desktop size**—24 inches in width and 20 inches in depth.

■ **General illumination.** Light brings your kitchen to life. A generous amount of light—both natural and artificial—reduces eyestrain while cooking or cleaning, and enables you to see inside cabinets and drawers easily.

Lots of daylight helps make your kitchen especially bright and livable. Planning an eastern or southeastern exposure for your kitchen brings the morning sunlight and a sunny and cheerful start for your day. It also means that the hotter afternoon sun won't wilt your plans for a hearty evening meal. When planning your kitchen's windows, think about the exposures you have and which wall offers the best views. Classic kitchen planning calls for a generous window over the sink so that you can daydream while doing dishes.

Artificial light is an important part of your kitchen's plans. For general purposes, make sure there are at least 2 watts of incandescent light or ¾ watt of fluorescent light for each square foot of floor space.

■ **Task lighting.** Whether you're chopping vegetables, helping kids with homework, or carving a turkey, each activity requires concentrated lighting. Task lighting is especially important during the evening hours. Good task lighting should be directed at the work area but not harsh enough to cause glare or shadows.

For fluorescent lighting that runs underneath the upper cabinets, use 8 watts of light for every foot of

countertop. Run lighting strips over at least two-thirds the length of the counter. Mount the strips as close as possible to the *front* of the cabinets. For lighting above sinks and islands, use two recessed or track downlights, 15 to 18 inches apart, with 75-watt reflector flood bulbs. Or, use a fluorescent fixture totaling 60 watts.

For an eating area, use about 120 watts of incandescent or 32 to 40 watts of fluorescent lighting. For a pendant or chandelier, position the fixture about 30 inches above the tabletop; the fixture should be 12 inches narrower than the table's diameter.

■ **Accent lighting.** Plants, collections, and works of art are all focal points deserving of a spotlight. Track lights work well as accent lights, or a Pella® Bow or Bay window is a great way to create a light-filled nook for plants or special display items. □

A DIFFERENT TYPE OF FLOORING HELPS SEPARATE THE FAMILY AREA FROM THE KITCHEN, *RIGHT.* SUNLIGHT SHINING THROUGH A PELLA® DOOR AND LOTS OF WINDOWS BRIGHTENS THE SPACE.

THE SUNSPACE ADDITION *BELOW* PROVIDES ROOM FOR A CASUAL DINING AREA IN THIS REMODELED KITCHEN.

MAKE A SPLASH WITH A BEAUTIFUL BATH

Today's baths have come a long way from the spare, white-porcelain-and-linoleum cubicles of the past. Modern baths with their whirlpools and steam showers are spacious, sun-soaked rooms made for relaxing. If you're longing for a luxurious bathroom retreat, use this section to plan your pampering paradise.

COMPONENTS AND MATERIALS

Finding the right components and materials for your bath ensures that the space will live up to your expectations. This room is special, so don't limit selections to what's immediately available in the local home-center stores. Shop long distance with consumer publications that showcase the latest designs. Then contact the manufacturer for a distributor near you.

Consider the big-ticket essentials first: tubs, sinks, and toilets. Each is available in a variety of shapes, materials, and colors, and manufacturers offer different price and performance levels.

■ Porcelainized cast iron is a durable, attractive material that keeps water warm for a long time. A cast-iron tub is heavy and may need extra floor support.

■ Enameled steel isn't as tough but is lightweight and great for remodeling.

■ Vitreous china's lustrous surface cleans well, but can chip when struck.

■ Fiberglass-reinforced plastic is light, warm to the touch, inexpensive, and molds into novel shapes. Abrasive cleaners may damage the surface.

When you choose fittings for your tub, shower, and sinks, pick faucets and shower heads that are eye-catching and mesh with the bath design. Function is very important: With today's emphasis on water conservation, you want efficiency as well as smooth operation.

Surface materials are your next consideration. Floors and countertops must be more than decorative; they must be easy-care and durable. Don't let the emphasis on utility scare you, though. You'll find surfaces that are every bit as attractive as they are practical.

Ceramic tile, for example, is the classic choice for bathroom floors, walls, and counters. It's impervious to water and lasts a lifetime. And, the variety of colors, shapes, and hand-painted designs offers endless creative possibilities.

Also, watch for the new solid, nonporous surfacing materials available for countertops, walls, and tub and shower surrounds. These tough and durable materials resist scratching, mildew, and moisture.

Once you've chosen components and materials, you're ready to plan your new bathroom's layout.

SUNLIGHT, MOONLIGHT, A WOODED VIEW—DRAMATIC PELLA® WINDOWS OVER THE WHIRLPOOL *OPPOSITE* DRAW IT ALL INDOORS.

HIGH CEILINGS AND HANDSOME WINDOWS ADD ARCHITECTURAL IMPACT TO THIS LUXURY BATH *BELOW.* IN THIS RESTFUL SETTING, WHO COULDN'T RELAX MIND AND MUSCLES?

GREAT SPACE STRATEGIES

Togetherness . . . it's wonderful, except when you're vying for the same spot at the bathroom mirror. Relax—you don't need a lot of space for the lavish his-and-her bath of your dreams. To garner more elbowroom, all it takes is some clever floor-plan tactics, and your double vision will be reality soon.

And, it doesn't matter whether you're remodeling or building, you can have a hand in laying out your new bath.

On graph paper, make a scaled drawing of the room where your bath will be. Using an accurate ruler, a clear plastic triangle, and a T square, include dimensions and locations of doors and windows. Note directions that doors swing. (Remember, if you're remodeling, it's much cheaper to locate a new bathroom near existing plumbing and your home's vent stack.)

Cut out to-scale patterns, or templates, of the fixtures you want to include in your bath. Don't leave anything out: double vanities, a roomy shower, a whirlpool bath for two, whatever you're wishing for. This is the part where you dare to dream and work at fitting it all in. Observe the Standards and Clearances on the next page and simply move the templates around on the scaled floor plan. If you're working with an architect's plan for a new house, position the templates in various locations to help you develop alternate ideas.

If there doesn't seem to be space for all the pieces, look beyond the obvious.

Here are some space-saving ideas:
- Place vanities back to back.
- Experiment with smaller size components. A less roomy tub? How about pedestal sinks instead of vanities? Or consider tubs, sinks, and showers that fit neatly into corners.
- If more room would solve your bathroom woes, take an inventory of the space around your bathroom for possible expansion. Enlarge the space by slicing a few feet from adjoining areas.
- Squeeze a hallway.

If space isn't a problem, you'll have even more flexibility in amenities: Include privacy walls between fixtures or establish independent grooming and bathing areas. You may also want a makeup center, a place to exercise, or a walk-in closet and dressing area.

Be sure to run your ideas by an architect or builder to determine if your plan is feasible and complies with building codes.

DESPITE THIS
BATH'S MODEST
DIMENSIONS,
OPPOSITE, THE
DESIGNER FIT IN
EVERY LUXURY.
THE BACK-TO-BACK
VANITIES *RIGHT*
TAKE UP LITTLE
FLOOR SPACE AND
LET TWO PEOPLE
PREPARE FOR THE
DAY AT THE SAME
TIME. THE CUSTOM
UNIT ALSO
PARTITIONS THE
BATHING AREA
FROM THE
GROOMING
CENTERS.

A CLEVER FLOOR
PLAN, *BELOW,*
MAKES THE MOST
OF THIS 10×10-
FOOT BATH. THE
HIGH CEILING
HELPS CREATE A
MORE SPACIOUS
FEELING IN THE
BATH BY ADDING
CUBIC VOLUME.

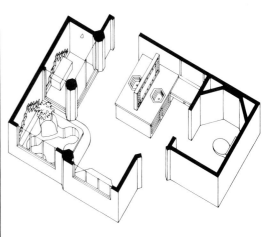

STANDARDS AND CLEARANCES

Even top-of-the-line bathroom fixtures won't serve you well if you don't allow yourself enough room to move around them easily. Allow maximum distances between fixtures if possible.

SINKS
■ Bowls range in size from 12×31 inches to 22×44 inches. Larger sizes are generally more comfortable to use and can minimize the amount of water splashed onto the floor.
■ Countertops are usually 31 to 34 inches high, although 36-inch counters are better for taller people. Two vanities allow you to individually customize counter height.
■ If you install two sinks in the same countertop,

allow a minimum of 12 inches between the sinks and at least 8 inches at each end of the countertop.

TOILETS
■ Twelve inches is usually the distance from the wall to the center of a toilet's floor flange. In the past, 5 gallons of water per flush has been typical— but most manufacturers now offer water-saver models that use 3½ gallons or less and help cut water costs. Water-saver toilets usually feature a low profile that opens up wall space for shelving.
■ Toilet seats are normally 14 inches high. For the disabled, an easier-to-use model is 18 inches high. Grab bars securely fastened to the wall aid the disabled.

TUBS AND SHOWERS
■ Standard tubs are 5 feet long and 30 inches wide, but they come as long as 6 feet. Tubs are increasingly available in a wider range of sizes and shapes, from square to oblong, oval to round.
■ Ordinary shower stalls range in size from 32 inches square up to 48 inches square. A comfortable minimum is 36 inches square.

TOWEL BARS
■ Each person using the bath needs at least 36 inches of towel bar. Hand towels fit on bars 18 inches long, and bath towels require bars at least 24 inches long.
■ Hang towel bars 36 to 42 inches from the floor.

Now you can take stock of all the necessities you use in your bathroom. It's no wonder that there never seems to be enough storage. But if you search your bath for unused space, you can capitalize on it. For example, niches beside the tub and inside the shower are ideal for storing toiletries where you need them.

Keep in mind that how you incorporate the storage depends on how presentable your bath items are and how accessible you want them to be.

For seldom-used items, consider building cabinetry above the bathtub. Or, build shallow shelves on the wall behind the bathroom door. To display stacks of colorful towels and other items, install shelves on a prominent wall.

Consider using furniture as storage units. An armoire makes an attractive addition to a bath and provides plenty of shelf or drawer space.

THE GOOD LIFE

Builders and designers report there are three things that almost everyone wants in a well-appointed bath: amenities, amenities, and . . . more amenities. A little bit of bathroom luxury can help begin your morning on an upbeat note or rejuvenate your spirits at the end of a long day. Special bathroom extras also have a very positive effect on the resale value of your home.

For a pampered shower, try multiple shower heads that give you an allover body massage. If you love a long soak in the tub, look to tubs fitted with

whirlpool jets. Heat lamps and towel warmers near the tub and shower will make for a toasty exit. A special window, such as a circlehead or an ellipse, will add a regal touch to your well-dressed bath.

SAFETY

■ Choose door hardware that can be unlocked from both sides in case you need to get in to rescue a child or injured person.

■ To prevent falls, choose slip-resistant flooring or install mats or traction strips, particularly in front of the sink, tub, or shower, where splashes may be common. Embossed rubber is so slip-proof and durable, it's often used in airports and malls. Secure area rugs with nonslip pads or double-face tape. It also helps if you have a good system for ventilating steam to prevent slippery condensation on the floor.

■ Shop for tubs with interiors that have flat bottoms and molded-in abrasive strips for sure footing. If you like the idea of a tub within a platform or recessed into the floor, consult architectural standards to design steps or ledges that have accessible, not awkward, dimensions.

■ Select tub and shower doors that are made of impact-resistant safety glass or plastic. Install hinges for swinging tub and shower doors on the end that is opposite control valves. Choose shower fittings that are shatter resistant and have rounded edges.

■ To avoid injury, set the water temperature no higher than 120 degrees. If you want hotter water for laundry and dishes, choose appliances with booster heaters. Or, faucets are available that automatically regulate water to a particular temperature.

■ Codes require that all bathroom electrical outlets feature ground fault circuit interrupters (GFCIs), devices that guard against shocks.

MAKE ROOM FOR A SPACIOUS TUB WITH A WINDOW-WRAPPED BUMP-OUT BAY, SUCH AS THIS ONE. AN ARCHED ENTRY, COLUMNS, AND ITS OWN SET OF STEPS GIVE THE NICHE A SENSE OF STYLE AND SECLUSION.

Photograph: Melanie Taylor Architecture. © 1991 Tom Yee

DESIGN TIPS AND TRICKS

A bath is the most personal room in your house, so let it express a mood that makes you comfortable. Color, pattern, and light all play a part in creating the atmosphere you want.

Now that bathrooms moonlight as dressing rooms, private saunas, and in-home spas, color has become as important as function. While high-tech devices such as whirlpools relax the muscles, simple color can act to soothe the mind. And, it's the combination of color and style that makes the mood for a room. For example, soft tones and traditional appointments create romance. Earth tones and country accessories add up to a rustic setting; bright colors with sleek, contemporary fixtures make a bold decorating statement. Darker colors, geometric shapes, and dramatic contrasts create a more masculine look; a subtle blend of pastels is more feminine.

Color can also alter how large your bathroom "feels." To make your bath seem bigger, select a one-color scheme for walls, counters, and fixtures. Dark shades and intricate patterns make rooms appear cozier.

High ceilings are another architectural asset, providing additional vertical space and making small spaces seem large by increasing cubic volume. Direct viewers' gazes upward with wood moldings, wallpaper borders, and vertically striped wallpaper or tile. Those same fool-the-eye techniques will lift a ceiling of standard height, too.

Other factors affect your bath's spatial qualities. If you want to open up space, then rule out wallpapers with busy pattern, bulky moldings, frilly window and shower curtains, or furry bath mats.

Mirrors and metals, materials with a reflective quality, stretch space by reproducing it. Mirrors are especially magical. Two mirrors positioned opposite each other create the illusion of a never-ending room. Mirroring the long wall of a narrow bath changes the room's proportions and makes it seem wider. Remember, place mirrors so they reflect the bath's assets, whether it's a tile mural, a panoramic view, or the widest room angle.

Windows bring a wonderful freshness

and vitality to the bathroom. If your privacy allows, consider replacing small windows with larger expanses of glass. An elegant Pella® Bow or Bay window, placed even with the height of the tub, provides a sunny nook for plants and bath accessories. Windows of different shapes—such as a half-round or ellipse—can give even the smallest bathroom a sense of character. Windows high on bathroom walls gather up light and maintain privacy.

SKYLIGHTS

Bringing sunshine into the bath makes it an even better place to relax. But not all baths feature gorgeous views or even exterior walls. Here's where a Pella Skylight can provide sunny solutions.

Skylights are a great way to beam brightness into your bath but still keep your privacy. Placed over a shower area, a Pella Skylight will cover your morning shower with a canopy of blue skies. Installed over a tub, a skylight lets you relax in your evening bath to a view of twinkling stars. Special options, such as Slimshade® blinds or Pleated Shades, add

MIRRORS, AN ALL-GLASS SHOWER SURROUND, AND PASTEL ALL PLAY IMPORTANT ROLES IN MAKING THIS BATHROOM *LEFT* SEEM MUCH LARGER THAN IT REALLY IS.

A ROUND SKYLIGHT ECHOES THE SHAPE OF THE CIRCULAR SHOWER IT ILLUMINATES, *RIGHT.* THE SHOWER CAN ALSO BE USED AS A LARGE SOAKING TUB.

a decorator touch and let you fully control sunlight.

ARTIFICIAL LIGHTING

Incandescent or fluorescent lighting plays a major role in a decorator's bag of tricks, and it is an important part of tasks such as shaving and applying makeup. You can use artificial lighting as an aid for everyday grooming and to highlight your bath's best features.

When you go to a showroom to select bathroom lighting, take along a rough sketch including room dimensions, ceiling height, window locations, special architectural details in the room, and a list of exercise or relaxation equipment to be installed. Your dealer can help you choose fixtures, but keep in mind a few fundamentals of good bathroom lighting:

■ In medium or large baths, a ceiling fixture centered over the front edge of the sink is a necessity.

■ Light a vanity mirror from each side or from both sides and the top.

■ In any separate areas, such as storage closets for exercise gear or a walled-off toilet, you'll need a ceiling fixture or wall bracket.

■ The tub or shower area requires a vaporproof recessed fixture.

These light tricks enhance space:

Push a bathroom wall out by bathing it in light. The effect can be achieved with wide-beam floodlights, wired into wall fixtures or ceiling tracks. Dark, shadowy corners and crevices tend to shrink a room. Illuminate those areas and the room will open up.

Select lighting fixtures for your bathroom with architectural design in mind. Elegant sconces, with an upward focus, highlight vertical space. Conceal a fluorescent light source behind a mirror. The light makes the mirror seem to float away from the wall. □

SUN-LOVING WAYS TO LIVE

HIGH CEILINGS AND PELLA® WINDOWS OPEN THIS LIVING ROOM *BELOW* TO SUNSHINE AND WARMTH.

Sunlight brightens our rooms, warms our bodies, and buoys our spirits. Most remodeling and building projects include plans to bring the marvelous magic of sunlight into our homes. Walls full of windows, stylish glass doors, bright skylights overhead, and cheerful sunrooms are just some of the ways you can add sunshine and livability to your indoor environment.

Not only are sun-filled spaces enjoyable, they're practical, too. Homes that scoop up sunshine take advantage of a free source of heat that can cut winter fuel bills. The principle behind this bright and energy-efficient way to live is called *passive solar design.* The theory is surprisingly simple. In fact, if you have south-facing windows or glass doors in your home, you already have the basis of passive solar design.

Passive solar design doesn't mean you must drastically alter the look of your home. Gone are the days of ungainly solar panels and mountains of sloped glass that make a house look like part of a science experiment. Today, good solar design simply means planning for south-facing glass to let in light from the low winter sun. Once inside, this sunlight not only brightens your days, but also turns into cozy warmth. In summer, when the hot sun moves high overhead, you can keep direct sunlight—and unwanted heat—from entering your home with

shades, blinds, trees, projecting eaves, or high-performance glass.

SUN-FILLED SUCCESS

Successful solar homes must be properly oriented to the sun. To put the power of

the sun to work in your new home or remodeling project, first determine whether solar design is practical in your part of the country. Check the *degree days* and *percentage of possible sunshine* for your area. Degree days measure how cold an area is. Refer to the map *opposite*

IN WINTER,
THE SUN'S RAYS
CAN PROVIDE
SOLAR WARMTH
FOR A HOME'S
INTERIORS, AS
SHOWN *BELOW*.

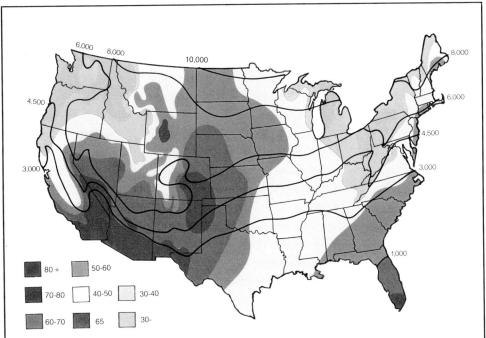

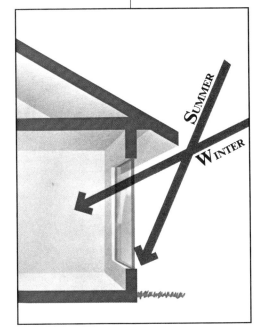

■ 80 +	■ 50-60
■ 70-80	□ 40-50
■ 60-70	■ 30-40
■ 65	□ 30-

to find your region's approximate degree days. The higher the number, the greater the likelihood that solar heating can help with energy bills.

Determine the percentage of possible sunshine using the map's color-coded key. If the measure for your area is lower than 50 percent, the energy gained by passive solar design will be minimal.

With this information as a guide, you can decide how worthwhile solar design is to you and your family. Although sunrooms and plenty of windows will always enhance the quality of your home's interiors, the orientation of your home or new addition toward the winter sun will be less important in some areas.

If you've decided that a solar design is a practical consideration for your new home or remodeling project, the next

step is to plan the site orientation. With a compass, stand on your building site and check which direction is south. This is the primary orientation for solar living, and your largest expanses of glass should face this direction. Note any trees that stand between you and south. Large evergreens such as pines or firs may block a significant amount of winter sun.

THIS SUN-
CATCHING DESIGN
ABOVE HAS A WIDE
FACADE AND
PLENTY OF PELLA®
WINDOWS.

THIS MAP *ABOVE*
SHOWS DEGREE
DAYS AND THE
PERCENT OF
POSSIBLE
SUNSHINE IN
DIFFERENT
REGIONS. DEGREE
DAYS MEASURE
THE TOTAL HEAT
USED TO WARM A
HOUSE DURING A
YEAR. THE HIGHER
THE NUMBER, THE
MORE OF AN
ADVANTAGE A
SOLAR DESIGN
MAY BE. USE THE
COLOR CODING TO
DETERMINE
PERCENTAGE OF
SUNSHINE. LESS
THAN 50 PERCENT
MAY MAKE SOLAR
DESIGNS
INEFFICIENT.

103

At this point, you may wish to consult with an architect or designer on an hourly fee basis to help you refine your basic plan. Most architects and designers are well aware of the advantages of passive solar design. For example, a good designer might suggest placing your garage on the north side of your home as a windbreak for cold winter breezes. Or, if your home is being built from stock blueprints, flopping the plan might be the best way to take advantage of solar orientation.

When planning a new home or large remodeling project, keep your solar design in mind. Active living spaces, such as the living room, dining room, and family room, should be on the south side of the house, where they will benefit directly from the sun's warmth. Spaces that produce heat, such as bathrooms or utility areas, can be located on the north side of the house so that their warmth balances sun-generated heat.

MADE IN THE SHADE

Having delightful, sun-filled rooms in the winter can banish cabin fever in even the coldest regions. In the warmer months, however, you'll need to make sure your home's interiors are protected from strong sunlight that can make air-conditioning costs skyrocket. As with all passive solar design principles, the solutions are simple.

■ **Landscaping.** Deciduous trees—trees that lose their leaves in autumn—are wonderful partners in passive solar

A SMALL PELLA® SUNSPACE CAN OPEN UP AN ORDINARY KITCHEN WITH A WIDE-EYED VIEW OF THE WORLD, *LEFT*.

A HANDSOME PELLA SUNROOM, *RIGHT*, CAN BE DESIGNED TO MATCH YOUR HOME'S EXTERIOR. DOUBLE-COATED LOW-EMISSIVITY GLASS FILLED WITH ARGON GAS HELPS CONTROL HEAT LOSS IN WINTER AND HEAT GAIN IN SUMMER.

THE SOUTH-FACING LIVING ROOM *OPPOSITE* TAKES FULL ADVANTAGE OF WINTER SUNLIGHT AND SPECTACULAR VIEWS WITH A WALL FULL OF PELLA WINDOWS.

ally of the homeowner. They help by blocking brisk winter winds that can rob a house of heat.

■ **Eaves and overhangs.** Many styles of houses make use of eaves—overhanging extensions of the roof—to help keep rain and snow away from exterior walls and foundations. Eaves also work nicely with the principles of solar design. In summer, when the sun is high overhead, eaves help shade a house and prevent direct sunlight from entering windows. In winter, however, sunlight from the low sun can pass underneath a home's eaves and help heat the interiors.

Remember that an eave can't protect against the late afternoon sun of the summer. For that you'll have to plan a method of shading. Exterior awnings or shutters work, but they can be ungainly. Interior blinds, shades, or curtains also block the sun, but only after its rays have already passed through the glass and entered your home, producing unwanted heat.

Pella® Slimshade® blinds and Pleated Shades are an excellent solution. They actually fit between the glass of the Double Glazing Panel System, where they are protected from dust and dirt. Slimshade blinds and Pleated Shades are fully operable and provide great flexibility in controlling sunlight.

■ **Keep your cool with ventilation.** Properly ventilating your house will also help to keep your home cool. Equal-size windows on opposite sides of a house encourage breezes to move through. Depending on your floor plan, you may be able to create a *thermal chimney* effect, where cool air enters from an opening in the basement or first floor of the house and exits through clerestory windows, an operable skylight, or dormer windows on the roof. For a thermal chimney to work, stairwell doors

designs. Located near south- or west-facing glass, deciduous trees can block unwanted summer sunlight and flood the areas around your home with cooling shade. In the fall, when the sun starts to swing low on the horizon, deciduous trees shed their leaves, permitting sunlight to enter your home with its magic warming powers. Evergreens planted to the north are also a natural

105

should be open to stimulate an unimpeded airflow. Of course, you may want to place gates across stairwells if you have children or pets.

Casement and awning windows will provide excellent ventilation because almost 100 percent of their area is available for airflow when fully opened. Opening a casement window also enables you to catch breezes moving parallel to the window.

SOLAR LIVING AT NIGHT

Passive solar design doesn't stop working once the sun goes down. In fact, you can maximize the efficiency of your solar design by planning for *thermal storage*. This idea allows you to capture much of the sun's heat energy for use later in the night—when you really need it.

Although thermal storage sounds as if it is highly technical, it isn't. You won't have to go to great lengths to take advantage of its benefits. Just be aware of what thermal storage means, then see if it can be part of your design plans.

Thermal storage means that things warm up when exposed to a source of heat. Any material inside your home is capable of providing thermal storage— your floors, walls, furniture, even the books on your shelves. Of course, some materials are much better at storing heat than others. Dense materials such as rock, brick, or concrete are the best.

Good thermal storage not only gathers heat, it releases it very slowly. Thus, when the source of heat is removed, as

when the sun sets or a thermostat is turned down, the storage material begins to release some of its heat like a radiator.

To use the principle of thermal storage, plan interior rock or masonry walls, or concrete slab floors covered with tile where they can receive direct sunlight. A brick wall at the back of a Pella® Sunroom or a massive stone fireplace exposed to southern sunlight will incorporate thermal storage in your design plans.

HIGH TECH AND HANDSOME

Great-looking Pella products offer many glazing and product options that can make sun-loving home designs and sunspaces comfortable and efficient. Low-emissivity glass, for example, helps

THIS BRIGHT, SUNNY KITCHEN *LEFT* INCLUDES THE ULTIMATE IN CONVENIENCE: A LONG EXPANSE OF PELLA® CASEMENT WINDOWS AND SKYLIGHTS WITH SLIMSHADE® BLINDS. SLIMSHADES ALLOW YOU TO CONTROL SUNSHINE AND HEAT GAIN.

to block the sun's damaging ultraviolet rays. At the same time, low-E glass reflects heat to keep it outside in summer and locked inside in winter. Optional high-performance, argon-filled, double-coated low-E insulating glass is filled with inert argon gas to raise its insulating capabilities.

For comfort and convenience, nothing quite matches the unique Pella® Double Glazing Panel System. This energy-efficient glazing option is available for most Pella products. It creates a $^{13}/_{16}$-inch air space between two layers of glass, a space big enough to permit the installation of adjustable Slimshade® blinds, Pleated Shades, or removable windowpane dividers. The Double Glazing Panel System can also be ordered with an optional high-performance low-E coating. For peak performance, Pella Type E Gold-tone Slimshade blinds reflect heat back into a room in winter, and can be used to keep out unwanted sun and heat in summer.

WINTERTIME, AND THE LIVING IS EASY

Sunrooms are some of the most popular ways to increase the livability of your home and take advantage of the benefits of solar design. A dazzling Pella Sunroom permits year-round living in the out-of-doors, all within the comfort and security of your home. Pella Sunroom glass lets in daylight but cuts down on unwanted heat loss or gain, and Pleated Shades and Slimshade blinds are available for both overhead and vertical glass surfaces to provide attractive ways to control privacy and comfort. Pella Sunrooms work readily with any architectural style, and a variety of sizes and combinations lets you add a sunny retreat to almost any room in your home. □

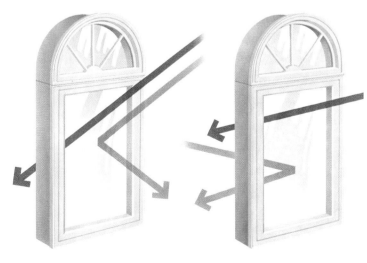

SUMMER   **WINTER**

A PELLA® SUNROOM BLENDS WITH A TRADITIONAL EXTERIOR, *ABOVE.*

LOW-E WINDOWS REFLECT HEAT TO THE OUTSIDE IN SUMMER AND INSIDE DURING WINTER, *LEFT.*

RISE 'N' SHINE ATTICS

Your search for more living space should be looking up. An unfinished attic may provide the space you seek at half the cost of an addition.

The results are often much more imaginative than other kinds of remodeling. Attic space frequently demands innovations, and the peak seems to inspire novel ideas, such as the colorful playroom *opposite*. "The whole feeling I wanted was like being in a circus tent," says Chicago-area homeowner Cathy Rosenbloom. Canvas tent flaps over the floor-to-ceiling Pella® windows are the perfect finishing touch.

Attics inspire more than playful whimsy. They seem to instill a sense of being literally above down-to-earth cares. Near their daughter's playroom, the Rosenblooms have a space of their own, a restful study. "At the end of the day, when the downstairs is a mess, we head up to the office," Cathy says. "It's so pretty at night, above the trees. . . ."

"ATTIC SPACES ARE THE BEST"

Cathy will get no argument from do-it-yourselfers Rick and Sandy Soria, of Des Moines. "Attic spaces are the best," says Sandy. "We walk up those steps and it's instant relaxation."

The Sorias moved into a home with no family room but with space overhead.

"The attic seemed the perfectly logical place to create the kind of kick-back-and-put-your-feet-up room that we wanted," says Sandy, who refers to the result of their remodeling as "our little treetop getaway."

CHECKING YOUR ATTIC'S POTENTIAL

The first step is to take a flashlight and a measuring tape up to your attic and check out dimensions and structural framework. Here's what to look for.

If your roof is held up by rafters, with open space beneath, the attic may be a remodeling candidate. If, however, you find a web of W-shape trusses supporting your roof, go back to planning that backyard addition because the attic isn't going to work out.

Another obstacle to your remodeling

plans may be the pathway to your attic. Trapdoors and ladderlike stairs are better for aerobics than for attics. You may have space to add a proper stairway: Plan on using a 3 × 13-foot space for conventional stairs, rising at a comfortable 30- to 35-degree slope and with at least 78 inches from any step to the ceiling above it.

Short on room? Here's a twist: Consider a spiral stairway. Spiral stairs require only a 5-foot circle of space.

OK, WE'RE UP HERE; NOW WHAT DO WE DO?

So, your roof is rafter-supported and you can have adequate attic access, it's time to stretch—not to see how fit you are but to see how you fit. Knock down the cobwebs and see how much usable space you have to work with.

EXPOSED COLLAR BEAMS, *OPPOSITE*, LET WINDOWS AND WALL SURFACES RISE ALL THE WAY TO THE ROOF PEAK.

SUNLIGHT POURS INTO AN ATTIC OFFICE, *LEFT*, THROUGH A PELLA® CIRCLEHEAD WINDOW AND SKYLIGHT.

Let's take it from the top: Measure your maximum headroom, from floor to the ridgeboard (a structural member positioned at the high point of the roof). If this distance is 10½ feet or more, there's enough headroom to meet common building code requirements.

In most areas, building codes specify that a living space must be at least 7½ feet high over 50 percent of the floor area. Plan to wall off those low-ceiling areas around the perimeter of your attic to increase the percentage of floor space that meets the height standard.

STRUCTURAL CHANGES

The final tests of an attic's conversion potential involve its structural adequacy. First, consider the floor joists—the wooden structure that holds up the attic floor and the ceiling beneath it. In some houses, attic floor joists are sized and spaced the same as lower floor joists (you can see *those* overhead from the basement). Usually, however, attic joists are lighter and farther apart and able to support less weight. If that's the case, you'll need to fortify them.

To determine if your joists are strong enough, measure their size, their distance apart, and their span from bearing wall to bearing wall. Compare your findings with local building codes. If you are unsure of your findings, consult a contractor or building inspector.

You can beef up joists by nailing

larger joists alongside them as reinforcement. Simply nailing a plywood subfloor over the joists does *not* strengthen the structural framework.

Consult a contractor or local-government building inspector to select the reinforcement's size. It's tricky: For instance, adding a 2×8 joist to a 2×4 joist gives *four* times the strength that you'd get by adding a second 2×4.

Building manuals, available at bookstores, usually provide useful tables that tell you how far a floor joist can safely span. A 2×6 joist supporting a floor should span no more than 8 feet from outside bearing wall to inside bearing wall; a 2×8 no more than 11 feet; and a 2×10 no more than 14 feet.

Also, look at the collar beams, those horizontal framing members that brace some of your rafters below the ridgeboard. If they are uncomfortably low, take heart: It's often possible to

DRAMATIC WALLPAPER, FLOWERED FABRICS, AND GAILY PAINTED COLLAR TIES TURN A SECOND-STORY ATTIC INTO A STORYBOOK BEDROOM, *RIGHT*.

TO KEEP A SMALL ATTIC COZY, NOT CROWDED, USE SHORT EDGE SPACES FOR SEATING AND SAVE THE TALL CENTER FOR WALKING HEADROOM.

SHED-ROOF DORMERS ARE GENERALLY LARGER THAN THE PEAKED GABLE TYPE, AND CAN RADICALLY TRANSFORM AN ATTIC SPACE— ESPECIALLY IF THE ROOF INCLUDES A SERIES OF PELLA® SKYLIGHTS.

can close up tight to create a snug and cozy upstairs room.

In most areas, building codes require that window area total at least 10 square feet or 10 percent of the room's floor area, whichever is greater. Windows also provide a means of emergency escape for attic bedrooms, so sills must be no higher than 44 inches above the floor.

Skylights offer some distinct advantages: They scoop in five times as much light as a sidewall window of the same size, without sacrificing privacy. Installed on a southside roof, skylights admit sunlight from the low winter sun and help cut heating costs.

Because ceiling surfaces are sometimes several feet from where your skylight is installed in the roof, you may need to construct a shaft to allow the light to reach your home's interiors.

■ Straight-shaft skylights use the same size opening in the roof as in the ceiling, connected by short walls called a shaft. The effect is like a spotlight, guiding sunlight where you want it.

■ To create a flared-shaft skylight, the hole through the ceiling is made larger than the size of the skylight. The result spreads a diffused light over a wide area.

■ A vaulted-ceiling skylight shaft lets in lots of light because the distance between the pitched ceiling and roof is minimal.

Today's Pella® Skylights offer superior performance with advanced engineering and weather-stripping techniques. Vented skylights provide fresh air at a touch, and energy-efficient accessories such as Slimshade® blinds or Pleated Shades give you state-of-the-art control over lighting and sun-powered heating.

You'll also have many options for creating your rooftop Windowscaping® designs. In the Sunbelt, for example, you

raise them. In some cases, you may need to add more collar beams to support an attic ceiling. Get professional advice, however, before you move or remove collar beams.

LIGHTENING UP AND GETTING IN SHAPE

Once you've determined that your attic meets the four criteria—rafter framing, adequate stairs, sufficient headroom, and sturdy joists—you're ready to consider ways to create an airy, light-filled retreat.

Sunlight and fresh air are priceless commodities for your attic remodeling project. You can't haul either one up the stairway, so plan to add operable windows and skylights. At a touch you can have the smell of spring blossoms or the sounds of evening crickets, or you

GABLE DORMERS CREATE DELICIOUS NOOKS, TUCKED IN UNDER THE EAVES AND SURROUNDING LEAVES. A DISTINCTIVE WINDOW IS THE PERFECT FOCAL POINT, INSIDE AND OUT.

may prefer custom-tinted glazing or a vent unit with built-in screen; in the North, count on triple weather stripping for a skylight that lets in sunlight without letting in the cold. Don't forget that Pella® Pleated Shades come in a variety of colors for just the right finishing touch in your upstairs retreat.

DORMER REFORMER

Dormer additions are a great way to add attic space without raising a big budget. The two basic types are gable dormers, like those shown on this page, and shed-roof dormers, shown on *page 112*. Any dormer will help stave off the tunnel syndrome that afflicts so many long, skinny attics. The gable style is generally perceived to be prettier, while the shed-roof style is more often a space-aiding workhorse. Of course, you'll want to think about the effect that a dormer addition will have on the exterior appearance of your house. Because constructing a dormer is not a job for the typical do-it-yourselfer, you'll need professional advice. Your architect or design/builder may be able to provide you with a sketch that will give you a preview of the finished job's appearance.

A light-filled dormer adds variety as well as space to your attic. "Attics are neat with their low spaces, especially for sleeping alcoves and study nooks," says Kansas City architect Fred Myers. "But, if there's no break in the space, you can get a claustrophobic feel."

Discussions of attics always get back to their "feel." Bob Hindson, one of Myers' clients, is delighted by the bedroom and sitting room that Myers designed for the attic of his Kansas City bungalow. Before remodeling, Bob says, going home had little appeal to him. "Now I look forward to it. The upstairs has *become* my home; I live up there." And that's a nice feeling. □

SIZING UP ATTIC POTENTIAL

So you've got the space, the cash, and the goal. Are you ready to go ahead with an attic remodeling? Well, maybe. Here's how to appraise your attic's finishing potential.

MAX HEADROOM
To be considered for remodeling, an attic needs about 10 feet of headroom at the peak. Requirements vary, but generally half of the *finished* attic area must be at least 7½ feet high.

STAIRING AHEAD
You may need to improve or relocate the entrance to your attic.
■ Allow at least 3 × 10 feet for a standard stairway, a 5½-foot circle for winding stairs.
■ To make room, look for a closet you can cut down; tuck spiral stairs in a corner or dormer.

STRUCTURED LIVES
Ask an architect or building contractor to check the joists for strength and movement. If the floors yield much, expect to reinforce the joists. For reinforcement, double up each joist—especially where they extend for long distances or support heavy objects.

HEATING UP
Don't trust the hot-air-rises principle to keep your attic warm.
■ If you have a forced-air heating system, extend ducts from the level below.
■ Auxiliary electrical units are a simple way to cozy-up the upstairs.
■ You may also need to reinsulate if your top insulation was in the attic floor.

UP TO CODE
Your plans aren't yours alone. Local government is sure to take an interest in your remodeling. Make sure your plans meet all building, electrical, and fire codes.

STEPS TO GREAT BASEMENTS

Forget any uneasy feelings you've ever had about basements. The space is *yours,* and it can be what you want to make it. Whether you're building a new home or looking for space to expand an old one, your basement is a buried treasure; the secret to finding its riches involves just a few key steps. These pages are the treasure map that will set your steps in the right direction.

SEEING THE LIGHT IN YOUR BASEMENT

Basements are often seen in 3-D, only here the three dimensions are Dark, Dank, and Dingy. Overcome this common misconception and you can add valuable living area to your home. The result is well worth the time it takes to evaluate your basement's potential and plan for finished rooms.

■ **Darkness.** Proverb writers and lyricists will tell you it's better to light one little candle than to curse the darkness. That solitary candle won't cut it in the world of basements. You need LIGHT, lots of it—all you can get from outdoors, and all you can add from electrical fixtures.

Start your plans by thinking about windows. Your goal should be to maximize the amount of daylight available to your basement. Don't restrict yourself to the tradition of small

windows marching around the top of your basement walls. With a mix of imagination and excavation, you'll see the light. For example, digging window wells can help bring in vast amounts of light. Plan to excavate far below the lower edge of your window so that you can fill the hole with drainage rock and gravel. A contractor or designer can advise you if a more sophisticated drainage system can be installed for your window well.

A daylight basement is easy to develop on a sloping lot. With careful attention to drainage, you can gain the same brilliant benefits anywhere. Here's proof, *right* and *below:* a belowground room that reaches out to sunlight. The

PELLA® WINDOWS AND DOORS BRING SUNNY BRILLIANCE TO A REMODELED BASEMENT, *RIGHT.*

THE DRAIN AT THE BASE OF THE BASEMENT ENTRY *BELOW* MAKES SURE THAT PATIO RUNOFF WILL NEVER BE A PROBLEM.

sunroom bump-out, 8-foot ceiling, and mirror wall add a spacious feeling.

If your basement will be used for sleeping, building codes typically require windows that are at least 2 feet wide and 3 feet high, with the sill no more than 44 inches off the floor. That's minimal; if your professional adviser says the wall won't be weakened, try to make the opening as wide as possible.

■ **Dank dismay.** Basement construction has been described as digging a well and then trying to keep the water out. Still,

dampness doesn't have to put a damper on your plans. To test for dampness, tape a mirror facing the wall. If moisture condenses on the mirror, through-wall dampness is the culprit. The cause is hydrostatic pressure, which increases during the rainy season and can actually force groundwater through pores in the foundation.

The solution is to make sure that rainwater or melting snow from your roof and yard is kept away from the foundation. First, check that each

AT *RIGHT* AND *BELOW:* THE BASEMENT GROUND RULES— MULTIPLE WINDOWS, OPEN SPACE, LIGHT- COLOR WALLS, BRIGHT-COLOR ACCENTS, WITH AMPLE TRACK AND RECESSED LIGHTS.

downspout has an extension and that the soil slopes away from the house.

If your site has a high water table, making wetness a chronic problem, then the best defense is a good offense. If water isn't oozing through pores but is pouring through cracks, plug the leaks with quick-setting cement. Talk to your contractor about sump pumps and drainage tile systems. These remedies often turn puddle-prone basements into completely dry living areas, and most remodeling contractors are familiar with installing these kinds of systems. In many new homes with basements, sump pumps are a standard feature.

■ **Down with dingy.** Adding sunlight and banning moisture can be extensive, expensive endeavors. But after tackling dark and dank, dingy is a fun challenge. The first rule: Forget any basement stereotypes. Use "upstairs" materials like drywall and recessed lighting. And don't forget insulation. Whether you use rigid foam panels or soft batts, plan for an insulation value of R-7 in areas where winters are mild, R-11 for harsher climates. Soft insulation usually is rated

at about R-3 per inch, so you can gauge your needs accordingly.

Use drywall on your outside walls, but don't be so hasty with room divisions. Because sunlight is so scarce in basements, "divide and conquer" is a poor strategy for floor plans there. Full-wall divisions limit the range that sunlight can reach. Instead, use grids, open shelving, or half walls to separate basement areas. A small, isolated room may seem cozy upstairs, but it will feel like a bunker in the basement. An open floor plan works best, so give your basement your undivided attention.

While there is no substitute for the vitality of sunlight, good electrical lighting can help. Use several recessed lights to brighten the area, then add bright task lighting where you need it. Finally, emphasize the area's best features with high-intensity accent lights.

When it comes to finishing your new space, save the earth tones for rooms above the earth. Below-grade areas are a good place for light backgrounds and brightly colored accents.

BOUNTIFUL BENEFITS FROM BEAUTIFUL BASEMENTS

Earth-sheltered housing, which captured attention in the energy-anxious '70s, cast subterranean living in a whole new light. Basements gained technology and acceptance. They have always had certain advantages: They're cool in the summer, safe in a storm, and relatively draft-free. Home handyfolk have long recognized the basement as a space bonanza. Now, with superior windows and finishing materials, the basement is rising to its rightful place as a valuable, cohesive part of the family home.

HOW TO SIZE UP YOUR BASEMENT

Before casting your basement in the challenging role of living space, let's take a close look at its qualifications. Some basements, unfortunately, are best left to workshops, storage, and the catch baskets of laundry chutes. How about yours? Consider these points.

GOT ENOUGH HEADROOM?

■ The minimum needed for comfort and building codes is 7½ feet. Even if you aren't extremely tall, you'll quickly feel claustrophobic if you have to scrunch under anything lower.

■ Pipes and heating ducts might dip lower, but you can cope with such shortfalls by placing low-profile furnishings beneath the low points.

ON THE LIGHT SIDE

■ Tiny windows at ceiling level may satisfy codes, but not comfort. Add more if the space is to feel like home.

■ Is there room for the broader, deep window boxes you'll need to bring daylight into the basement?

PUTTING ON AIRS

■ Ventilation is a key difference between a musty cellar and a must-see basement. Windows will help with ventilation, but you need to assess the heating and cooling system, too.

■ Keep the position of vents in mind as you plan your improvements, and be prepared to add to your system.

NOTHING SUCCEEDS LIKE ACCESS

■ The best basement will never offer true living space if you have to open a trapdoor in the garage to get there. Plan wide steps that conform to your local codes. A landing at the top of the stairs prevents having to open a door directly onto a descending stairway.

■ Safety demands a second basement exit, preferably a large and easily opened window.

CRAFTED WITH CARE

THE CURVE OF PELLA® ARCHITECT SERIES ARCH CASEMENT WINDOWS, *LEFT,* RECALLS THE MISSION STYLE OF ARCHITECTURE. THE NARROW WINDOWPANE DIVIDERS ARE A SPECIAL FEATURE OF THE ARCHITECT SERIES˜.

UNIQUE WINDOW AND DOOR CONFIGURATIONS CAN BE MADE IN THE CUSTOM SHOP, *RIGHT.* EACH CUSTOM PRODUCT IS CAREFULLY DESIGNED AND HANDCRAFTED.

O F ALL THE DECISIONS YOU WILL MAKE WHEN BUILDING or remodeling your home, choosing Pella® windows and doors may be the most satisfying. They look beautiful. They perform beautifully. And, as you'll discover on the following pages, the Pella/Rolscreen Company goes to extraordinary lengths to ensure that all of its products give you lasting quality, season after season.

118

At Pella®/Rolscreen, every employee is dedicated to excellence and unsurpassed craftsmanship. That's why each year thousands of architects, builders, and homeowners trust Pella products to make their finest dreams come true. The familiar yellow-and-black Pella product label is an assurance of the quality and high standards that have become the hallmarks of the Rolscreen Company.

Every Pella product is backed by more than 65 years of experience in manufacturing state-of-the-art window and door systems. This experience is the backbone of a commitment to support design professionals, builders, and homeowners in every possible way. Few window and door manufacturers go to such great lengths to create a helpful nationwide network of service.

INNOVATION BUILDS A WINNING PHILOSOPHY

Pella/Rolscreen doesn't just build fine windows and doors, it constantly seeks to fulfill the needs and goals of builders and homeowners. This means that even though Pella design engineers have generated dozens of exclusive patent rights, they are never content to sit on their laurels. They study the effects of wind, rain, and seasonal changes so that they can create windows and doors that will last for generations. They subject windows and doors to harsh, rigorous tests to ensure that Pella products meet or exceed the industry standards for performance. And they are relentless in

their pursuit of ways to offer features of comfort and convenience to the homeowner.

Here are just some of the ways that Pella windows and doors provide superior performance:

■ **Easy wash feature.** All casement, double-hung, and awning windows allow exterior glass surfaces to be cleaned *from inside your home.* Gone are the days of strained necks and shaky extension ladders. Even your second-story windows are within easy reach.

■ **Extra-tough cladding.** Pella/Rolscreen believes that the best windows are made of wood, and the toughest exteriors are aluminum. Pella windows combine both components for peak energy efficiency and longevity. The exclusive Permacoat™ coating is available in a variety of colors and far exceeds the performance of paint alone. Permacoat resists chalking, fading, corrosion, and airborne pollutants.

■ **Hardy hardware.** Pella/Rolscreen hardware meets the same high standard⌐

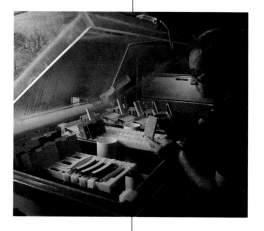

QUALITY IS THE PRIMARY CONCERN OF THE CAREFUL CRAFTSPEOPLE WHO ASSEMBLE WINDOWS IN THE CUSTOM SHOP, *OPPOSITE.*

PELLA® ENGINEERS USE A SPECIAL CHAMBER, *ABOVE,* TO CHECK THE RELIABILITY OF PERMACOAT™ CLADDINGS.

IF YOU CAN DREAM IT, CHANCES ARE IT CAN BE BUILT IN THE CUSTOM SHOP, *LEFT.*

as the rest of its products. For example, the gears of Pella® casement window operators are made of hardened metals that resist wear. There's even a hardware for lovers of oceans: seacoast hardware is especially resistant to the corrosive effects of salt mist and spray.

■ **Between the panes.** Many people love blinds or windowpane dividers but hate to clean them. So Pella/Rolscreen design engineers went to the drawing board. Their ingenious Double Glazing Panel System allows Slimshade® blinds, Pleated Shades, or wood windowpane dividers to be placed between two sheets of glass, away from dust and dirt. Special options include Type E Gold-tone Slimshade blinds that increase energy performance.

■ **Old-world elegance.** Some folks talked about the bygone days of traditionally elegant windows and doors. Pella/Rolscreen responded by creating one of the most beautiful and important product lines in the business: The Architect Series™. These exquisite windows and doors recall the grace and distinction of significant architectural periods such as prairie school and French colonial. Taking this idea one step further, Pella®/Rolscreen design engineers developed Integral Light Technology™. This revolutionary technology makes extremely narrow windowpane dividers possible, yet provides the strength, integrity, and look of true divided-light windows. Integral Light Technology also provides superior energy efficiency.

■ **Rolling screens.** This original invention, first developed more than 65 years ago, established Pella/Rolscreen as an innovative leader. The famous Rolscreen® rolling screen is available on casement windows, and allows the screen to glide up and out of sight to provide a crystal-clear view of the world.

A DEDICATED SYSTEM OF SERVICE

As proud as Pella/Rolscreen is of its fine products, it is just as proud of the network it has developed to bring excellent local service to its many customers. The foundation of this system is The Pella Window Store®. More than 400 Window Stores are located nationwide to place the expertise of trained Pella professionals right where they can do the most good—in your neighborhood. In addition to being showrooms for Pella products, Window Stores are resource centers where you can get answers to your questions about Windowscaping® designs, energy performance, standard features, and options.

Helping to complete the network of service is the Certified Pella Contractor (CPC) program. This innovative program allows you to select builders and remodelers who have been specially trained in the installation of Pella products. The CPC program is part of the nationwide effort to make sure your Pella products are installed and operate properly year after year. (See pages 76–77 and 80–81 to learn what Certified Pella Contractors say about building and remodeling projects.)

PELLA® DESIGN ENGINEERS, *ABOVE,* WORK HARD TO CREATE STATE-OF-THE-ART PRODUCT INNOVATIONS.

HANDS-ON CARE AND METICULOUS CRAFTSMANSHIP ARE THE HALLMARKS OF CUSTOM PELLA PRODUCTS, *RIGHT.*

Photograph: H. David Seawell/Westlight

*O*ur company was founded on the belief that a successful business should give customers honest value, provide opportunities for employees, and help make the community a better place to live and work. It goes back to the Dutch settlers who founded Pella, Iowa, in 1847. They brought with them a strong sense of pride in their work, home, and community that still thrives today.

This sense of pride has given Pella a worldwide reputation for quality, value, and beauty. It's a reputation we strive to uphold by making products that will make your home a better place to live. □

—**Wayne Bevis**
President, Rolscreen Company

ROLSCREEN COMPANY PRESIDENT WAYNE BEVIS TAKES A PERSONAL INTEREST IN UPHOLDING THE WORK ETHIC OF THE PELLA COMMUNITY. BEVIS, LEFT, TALKS OVER SOME FINE POINTS OF CUSTOM WINDOW CONSTRUCTION WITH ABE BOS.

124

INDEX

PELLA® DISTRIBUTORS

ALABAMA
J.F. Day & Company
Birmingham, AL
202/322-6776

Pella Windows and Doors, Inc.
Mobile, AL
205/666-6820

ARIZONA
Pella Windows and Doors, Inc.
Tempe, AZ
602/968-7841

ARKANSAS
Pella Products Company
North Little Rock, AR
501/758-5050

CALIFORNIA
Pella Products
Corona, CA
714/272-1700

Pella Architectural Products, Inc.
Downey, CA
213/803-4361

Pella San Joaquin
Fresno, CA
209/275-2624

Pella Company
North Highlands, CA
916/488-7888

Pella Sales Company
San Francisco, CA
415/648-8600

Pella Windows & Doors, Inc.
Spring Valley, CA
619/670-6528

COLORADO
Pella Products of Colorado, Inc.
Denver, CO
303/388-0884

CONNECTICUT
Pella Products Division
Robert Hunt Corporation
Hartford, CT
203/527-4732

FLORIDA
Pella Window & Door Co.
Jacksonville, FL
904/731-3655

Robert Hunt Corporation USA
Longwood, FL
407/831-0600

GEORGIA
Pella of Georgia
Lawrenceville, GA
404/339-8000

HAWAII
Pella Division J.B.L.
Hawaii, Ltd.
Honolulu, HI
808/847-4021

ILLINOIS
Illini Pella, Inc.
Champaign, IL
217/356-6474

Pella Windows & Doors, Inc.
Glendale Heights, IL
708/894-1000

Pella Window Company, Inc.
Milan, IL
309/787-4440

Pella Products, Inc.
Rockford, IL
815/397-6780

INDIANA
Pella of Evansville
Evansville, IN
812/423-6891

Irmscher Suppliers, Inc.
Fort Wayne, IN
219/456-4581

McComb Window & Door Co., Inc.
Indianapolis, IN
317/872-9927

South Bend Sash and Door Co., Inc.
South Bend, IN
219/287-2901

IOWA
Pella Co.
Des Moines, IA
515/278-8781

Pella Windows & Doors Corp.
Fort Dodge, IA
515/955-7080

Wilsey Company
Sioux City, IA
712/258-4567

Windows by Pella
Waterloo, IA
319/988-4200

KANSAS
Pella Products, Inc.
Hutchinson, KS
316/662-8276

Pella Windows of Kansas, Inc.
Topeka, KS
913/233-7454

KENTUCKY
Pella Products Corporation
Louisville, KY
502/491-1212

MARYLAND
James A. Cassidy Company, Inc.
Beltsville, MD
301/953-7700

MASSACHUSETTS
Pella Windows, Inc.
Fall River, MA
508/676-6820

Pella Products, Inc.
Greenfield, MA
413/772-0153

Pella Windows & Doors, Inc.
Wilmington, MA
508/658-6889

MICHIGAN
Horne Bldg. Specialties, Inc.
Grand Rapids, MI
616/949-2400

Pella Window and Door Company
West Bloomfield, MI
313/624-8080

MINNESOTA
The Pella Window Store
Hibbing, MN
218/263-8361

Pella Products, Inc.
Minneapolis, MN
612/623-7640

MISSISSIPPI
J.F. Day & Company
Jackson, MS
601/956-9544

MISSOURI
Pella Products Company
North Kansas City, MO
816/471-0414

Pella Products of St. Louis, Inc.
St. Louis, MO
314/645-5870

MONTANA
Pella Windows & Doors, Inc.
Billings, MT
406/656-1516

NEBRASKA
Central Nebraska Pella Products, Inc.
Grand Island, NE
308/384-0800

Pella Products of Omaha
Omaha, NE
402/331-9225

NEW JERSEY
Pella Windows & Doors
West Caldwell, NJ
201/575-0200

NEW MEXICO
Pella Rio Grande, Inc.
Albuquerque, NM
505/345-3501

NEW YORK
Westny Bldg. Prod. Corp.
Buffalo, NY
716/681-2000

Crawford Door & Window Sales
Rensselaer, NY
518/286-1900

The Maurer Company, Inc.
Rochester, NY
716/454-4990

Pella Window & Door Division
East Syracuse, NY
315/437-2717

NORTH CAROLINA
Pella Window and Door Co.
Greensboro, NC
919/379-8550

NORTH DAKOTA
Pella of North Dakota, Inc.
West Fargo, ND
701/282-9505

OHIO
Gunton Corp.-Ohio Division
Bedford Heights, OH
216/831-2420

Pella Marketing Systems, Inc.
Cincinnati, OH
513/489-8808

Pella Sales, Inc.
Kettering, OH
513/435-0141

Pella Products
Toledo, OH
419/385-7447

OKLAHOMA
Pella Products Division
Oklahoma City, OK
405/478-4350

OREGON
Pella Window and Door Company
Beaverton, OR
503/641-4622

PENNSYLVANIA
Pella Windows & Doors, Inc.
Dunmore, PA
717/346-7722

Gunton Corp.-Philadelphia Div.
Norristown, PA
215/631-9500

Gunton Corp.-Pittsburgh Div.
Sewickley, PA
412/741-8855

SOUTH CAROLINA
Pella Window and Door Company
Columbia, SC
803/754-5857

SOUTH DAKOTA
North Central Supply, Inc.
Rapid City, SD
605/341-2045

TENNESSEE
Tate Window & Door Co.
Knoxville, TN
615/588-9621

J.F. Day & Company
Memphis, TN
901/345-5760

Pella Window and Door Co.
Nashville, TN
615/256-8383

Pella Window Stores, Inc.
Paris, TN
901/642-2641

TEXAS
Willard Boswell Company
Arlington, TX
817/640-0486

Pella Windows & Doors
Houston, TX
712/896-6444

Pella Products of South Texas, Inc.
San Antonio, TX
512/735-2030

UTAH
Pella Intermountain
West Jordan, UT
801/566-4131

VIRGINIA
Pella Virginia, Inc.
Richmond, VA
804/275-7809

WASHINGTON
Pella Products
Spokane, WA
509/624-4281

Pella Windows & Doors, Inc.
Woodinville, WA
206/488-3004

WISCONSIN
Ver Halen, Inc.
Green Bay, WI
414/435-3791

WYOMING
Rex Robertson Company, Inc.
Casper, WY
307/234-1518

CANADA
Pella-Hunt Corporation
London, Ontario
519/686-3100

JAPAN
Daiken Trade & Industry Co., Ltd.
Toyama
0763-82-0304

C. Itoh Building Products Co., Inc.
Hawthorne, NY
914/347-5600

AUSTRALIA
Pella Australia PTY, Ltd.
Manuka, ACT
06-239-6568

BRITISH WEST INDIES
Kirkconnell Brothers, Ltd.
Grand Cayman, Cayman Islands
9-2521

*For areas not listed,
call 800/524-3700 for
more information.*

Before you build or remodel, make an addition to your library.

A limited hard bound edition of this glossy 128 page book is now available for just $6.95

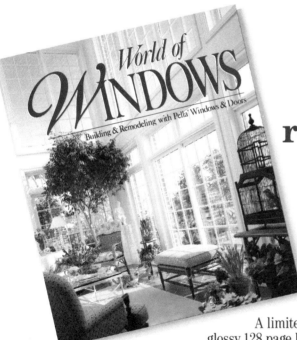

Before you build or remodel, make an addition to your library.

A limited hard bound edition of this glossy 128 page book is now available for just $6.95

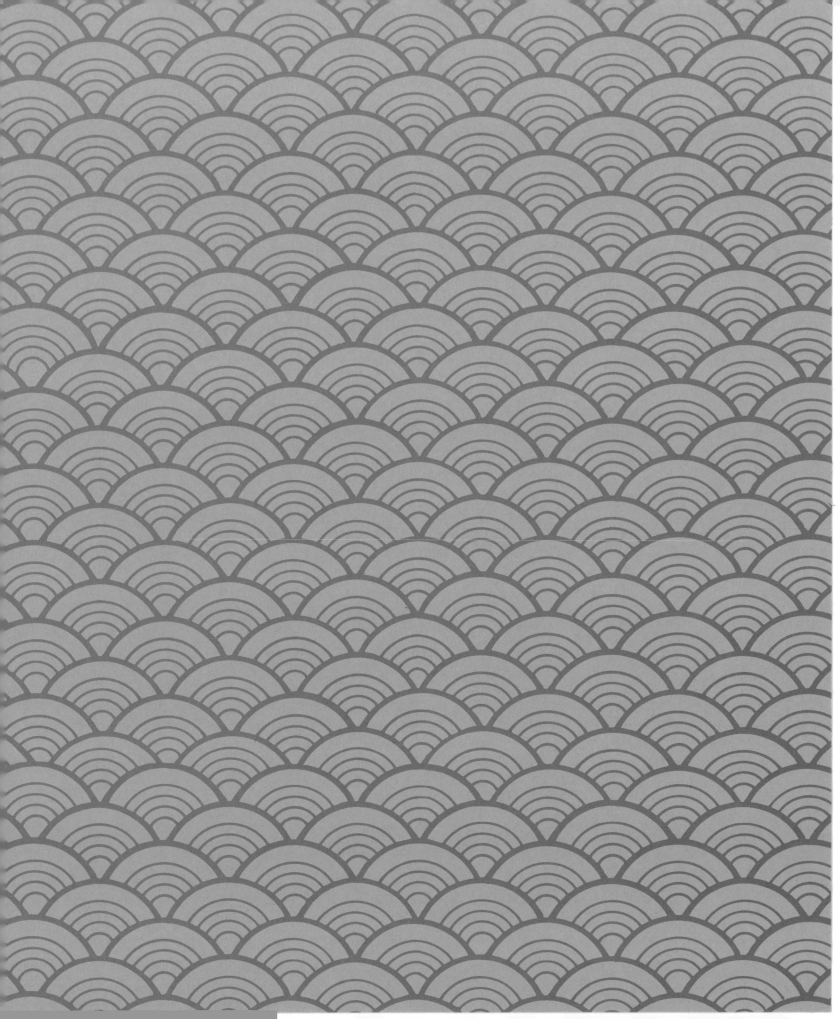